The Concise Legal Dictionary

1000 Legal Terms You Need to Know

By Richard Campbell

Minute Help Press

www.minutehelpguides.com

Table of Contents

1, 2 3

401(k) plan

for oh wahn kay plan

A type of retirement savings plan in the U.S. It lets workers keep funds that get invested but not taxed until they are withdrawn.

A

A fortiori
ah for-shee-O-ree; a for-she-O-rai
"From the stronger." Refers to arguments that apply with even greater force to one set of facts than to another. For example, if a standard baseball does not fit somewhere, then neither will a basketball.

A posteriori
ah pos-tee-ree-OH-ree; a pah-stee-ree-O-rai
"From the later." Inductive. Looking at particular events or results, and finding common causes or theories. *Compare with a priori.*

A priori
ah pree-O-ree
a PRAI-o-rai
"From the earlier." Deductive. Looking at general theories and causes, and finding particular effects or results. *Compare with a posteriori.*

Abandonment
ah-BAN-dun-ment
Leaving something or someone (or giving up rights to control), and intending to never reclaim the person or thing. Simply not using property is not abandonment.

Abatement
ah-BAY't-ment
Decrease, pause, or termination. For example, one might file a motion to abate a case until another case is finished. In wills, abatement means a decrease in money inherited because it was used to pay estate debts.

Abode
ah-BOW'd
One's home or usual residence. The place where one regularly spends the night or other frame of time. One way to serve court papers is to leave them with someone of suitable maturity at the defendant's abode.

Abstention
abs-TEN-shun
A federal court's disavowal of its power to hear a case. Federal judges may invoke abstention doctrines if necessary to avoid needless conflict with state officials.

Abstract
AB-strak't
Something that is theoretical and does not necessarily concern any specific factual situation. Also the name for a concise summary of a longer document.

Abuse of process

ah-BYOOS uhv PRAH-ses

Any use of legal procedures for a goal other than the one for which they are intended. One example is serving a subpoena just to scare someone.

Acceleration

ak-seh-leh-RAY-shun

Speeding up. In specific contexts:

(1) In contracts, the speeding up of due dates. Under a pre-agreed acceleration clause, the entire loan may become due immediately after a missed payment.

(2) In real property, a situation in which property rights change hands faster because of the failure of a prior estate.

Acceptance

ak-SEP-tens

Agreement to the terms of an offer. It must be communicated in a way required or allowed by the offer. A valid acceptance can sometimes add new or additional terms depending on the governing law.

Accession

ek-SEH-shun

An increase or addition to something. An accession of cash makes one wealthier. An accession to a contract means an agreement to join the contract.

Accessory

ak-SEH-so-ree

Someone who intentionally helps commit a crime or evade police, but is not present at the crime scene. Accessories before the fact help before the crime. Accessories after the fact help after the crime.

Accomplice

uh-KAHM-plis

Someone who intentionally helps another commit a crime or evade police. Acccomplice liability can lead to the same criminal punishment as given to principals in the first degree.

Accord and satisfaction

UH-kord and sa-tis-FAK-shun

A new agreement (accord) that discharges an old agreement (satisfaction). In the usual case, a conflict about the amount of money owed leads to an agreement that the debtor will pay a lower amount.

Account

ah-KAH-oont

(1) A detailed record of how much each party to a transaction owes the other. A bank account may be thought of as such record between a person and bank.

(2) A story or explanation for some event. Witnesses for each party in a case often give competing or contradictory accounts.

Accretion

ah-KREE-shun

Increase. Can refer to increase in property values, or natural addition of soil to land. In wills, refers to increases in the value of property before it is inherited.

Accrual method

ah-KROO-ahl MEH-thud

Accounting method that recognizes income when it is earned, without waiting for actual payment. Expenses are recognized as soon as debts arise.

Acquittal

ah-KWIT-uhl

A finding that one is not guilty of a crime. Often reached by a jury, but sometimes by a judge acting as fact-finder.

Action

AK-shun

A judicial proceeding, either civil or criminal in nature. The phrase "action at law" used to stand in contrast to the phrase "suit in equity." That distinction was abandoned in most jurisdictions of the U.S. *See* equity (def. 4).

Actual authority

AK-tchu-ahl uh-THO-reh-tee

Authority intentionally conferred by a principal on an agent, plus authority that the agent reasonably believes he or she acquired based on the principal's conduct.

Actual cash value

AK-tchu-ahl kash VAL-yoo

The cost to replace an item, minus the amount of money lost to depreciation from age.

Actual cause

AK-tchu-ahl kawz

A logical connection in which the existence of one fact creates another fact. Water in the air is an actual cause of snow. *See* but-for test.

Actus reus

AK-tus RAY'oos

The behavioral element of a crime. It refers to a physical act (or failure to act) that constitutes a crime when coupled with a certain mental state. *See mens rea*.

Ad hoc
ad hahk; ad hoh'k
"For this." Created for a particular purpose or reason. An *ad hoc* court may be created to deal with war crimes in a certain country.

Ad hominem
ad HAH-meh-num
"To the person." For example, an *ad hominem* response attacks the person who made an argument, rather than the argument itself.

Ad infinitum
ad in-fih-NAI-tuhm
"To infinity." Refers to the potential ability of a rule to continue producing results forever. For example, a statute might prescribe an additional year of jail for every $10,000 stolen *ad infinitum*.

Ad litem
ehd LAI-tem
"For the lawsuit." For example, a guardian *ad litem* may be appointed to represent the interests of a child in a court case. Such person then physically meets with any attorneys and other persons involved to safeguard the interests of the child.

Ad valorem tax
ad vah-LO-rum taks
A tax according to value. Calculated from the value of property, rather than its quantitity or type. Most often applied to real property taxes.

Additur
A-dee-toor
An increase in damages from the amount awarded by a jury. Trial courts may order additur instead of declaring a new trial due to inadequate damages.

Ademption
ah-DEMP-shun
Cancellation of a promised transfer by will because the property involved is not part of the testator's estate at death.

Adequate and independent state grounds
AEH-deh-kwut and in-duh-PEN-dent stayt GRAH-oonds
State laws that fully underpin a decision regardless of federal law. The U.S. Supreme Court will not hear an appeal from the highest state court if it rests on such grounds.

Adequate provocation
AEH-deh-kwut PRAH-vah-kay-shun
A necessary element of voluntary manslaughter. Requires that victim did something to sufficiently provoke

defendant into a sudden rage without time to cool off.

Adjudication
uh-joodee-KAY-shun

The process of judicially resolving a dispute. Administrative agencies hold adjudication hearings before issuing orders affecting specific parties.

Adjusted gross income (AGI)
ah-JUS-ted GROH's IN-kum (a jee ai)

Gross income minus any deductions allowed by tax laws. The goal is to deduct from one's taxable income the cost of earning that income.

Admissible
ad-MIH-sih-b'l

Permitted for consideration. For example, evidence that is not admissible cannot be considered by the jury at trial. Judges decide whether evidence can be admitted.

Admission
ah'd-MIH-shun

(1) Express confirmation during a court case that something asked about is true. For example, anything admitted during discovery need not be proven at trial.

(2) A statement made before a court case that now gains significance as a prior acknowledgement by a party of a now-relevant fact. Either not treated as hearsay or admitted despite being hearsay.

Adultery
uh-DOL-teh-ree

Open and notorious cohabitation or sexual relations with another person. In addition, either defendant must be married to a third party, or defendant must know that the other person is married to a third party.

Advance directive
ad-VAN's dih-REK-tiv

A document in which one legally expresses wishes about what is to be done in case of physical or mental incapacitation. *See* living will, durable power of attorney.

Adversary proceeding
ad-VUR-sa-ree

Formal dispute of legal claims between two parties in court. In bankruptcy law, refers to a specific dispute within the larger context of a bankruptcy proceeding.

Adverse possession
ad-VURS puh-ZEH-shun

Unlawful use of property that matures into legal title if the owner fails to sue within the statute of limitations. Use must be actual, hostile, open and notorious, exclusive, and continuous.

Affidavit
a-feh-DAY-vit

A person's voluntary statement, recorded in writing, and supported by an oath sworn before a notary public or someone else with authority to administer oaths.

Affirm
uh-FURM
To uphold or confirm something. An appellate court confirming a lower court's ruling may be said to affirm it. People can also affirm oaths instead of swearing to them.

Affirmative defense
uh-FUR-muh-tiv deh-FENS
A defense that leads defendant to victory even if all the allegations in plaintiff's complaint are true. Self-defense and insanity are common affirmative defenses.

Agency
AY-jen-see
(1) A type of government body that puts laws into effect and administers them. Administrative agencies are executive-branch institutions.
(2) A relationship in which one party (agent) acts on behalf of another (principal). The relationship may stem from contract or law, and imposes fiduciary duties.

Agent
AY-jent
Someone with authority to act in place of someone else. The person represented by an agent is called the principal.

Aggravating circumstance
A-grah-vay-ting SUR-kuhm-stans
A fact or reason that makes action more blameworthy, increases degree of liability, or leads to greater punishment. *See, e.g.*, first degree murder.

Agreement
AH-gree-ment
(1) Mutual understanding between multiple parties. Often used as a synonym for mutual assent.
(2) The bargain actually struck by different parties to a contract. Refers to the full meaning of the bargain, taking into account circumstances and definitions that may not have been formally recorded in the contract.
(3) Another name for a contract.

Alimony
A-lih-moh-nee
An allowance ordered to be paid by one spouse to another during separation, or after divorce. Should be based on the amount needed for maintenance and support.

Alternative causes
uhl-TUR-nah-tiv KAW-zez
Two or more facts that could have separately caused a result. Still, one or more was not a substantial factor. In tort cases, alternative-cause defendants often try to prove that they did not actually cause plaintiff's injury.

Alternative dispute resolution (ADR)

uhl-TUR-nah-tiv dis-PYOO reh-zuh-LYOO-shun (a dee ahr)

A way to resolve conflicts outside the court litigation process. Arbitration and mediation are the main processes used. Less rigid and often cheaper than litigation.

Ambiguous

am-BIG-yoo-uhs

Capable of being reasonably understood in two or more ways. If ambiguously written, a law or contract may be found void and have no legal effect.

Amendment

uh-MEND-ment

A change that officially deletes, modifies, or replaces something. A constitutional amendment changes the original text of the constitution. A statutory amendment changes the text of a legal rule.

Amicus curiae

ah-MEE-kuhs kyoo-REE-ai

"Friend of the court." Someone who voluntarily brings some information to the attention of a deciding court, while not actually being a party in the case.

Amount in controversy

EM-au-oon't in KAHN-trah-vur-see

The sum of money damages demanded by a plaintiff, or the dollar value of non-monetary relief. For diversity jurisdiction purposes, claims by different plaintiffs, or claims against different defendants usually cannot be added together.

Annuity

uh-NYOO-ee-tee

A stated sum of money that is paid at regular intervals, such as every month or year. Also the name for an obligation to pay such money, or a right to receive it.

Answer

AN-sur

The first pleading by a defendant that speaks to the merits of a case. Usually denies allegations, offers defenses, and expresses counterclaims.

Anticipatory repudiation

an-TEE-sih-pah-tory reh-pyoo-dee-AY-shun

A contracting party's conduct or words, expressed before performance is due, that indicate an intention not to perform. The other party is excused from performing and can immediately sue for damages.

Apparent authority

uh-PAR-ent uh-THO-reh-tee

Authority that is legally recognized even though not actually given. An agent's unauthorized actions will bind the principal if a third-party reasonably believes such authority existed based on the third-party's dealings with the princpal.

Appeal

AH-peel

Review of a lower court's decision to see if it should be overturned. In criminal cases, the first appeal usually exists as a right. Subsequent appeals are discretionary.

Appearance

ah-PEE-rens

Coming into court, either physically or by filing documents. The parties to a case, interested persons, and their attorneys are said to make an appearance.

Appearance of impropriety

ah-PEE-rens uhv im-proh-PRAI-ye-tee

Reasonable perception that something is unlawful or unethical. For example, judges with some connection to a party should sometimes recuse themselves to avoid the appearance of impropriety, even if not actually biased.

Appellate

ah-PEL-aht

Having to do with an appeal. A court that reviews a lower court's decisions is an appellate court. A brief discussing problems at trial and seeking reversal is an appellate brief.

Appropriation

ah-pro-pree-EY-shun

Taking control over property. A legislature using tax funds for a project is said to appropriate the money. In torts, appropriating someone's name or image means using it for monetary gain.

Arbitrary and capricious review

AHR-bit-ra-ree and cap-REE-shus ree-VYU

A legal test that applies to informal rulemaking of administrative agencies. Reviewed actions are upheld unless clearly based on a whim or prejudice.

Arbitration

ahr-bih-TRAY-shun

An out-of-court, binding process for resolving disputes. Decisions are made by one or more third-parties called arbitrartors. Some arbitrators are neutral; others are picked by a party to the dispute.

Arbitrator

AHR-bih-tray-tor

Someone who decides a dispute in arbitration. May serve alone as part of a panel. Can be fully neutral and new to the subject matter, or can be specifically picked by one or more parties for reasons that may include techncial expertise.

Arraignment

uh-RAY'n-ment

The first step in a criminal prosecution. It involves bringing the defendant to court, having the judge list the charges, and asking the defendant to enter a plea.

Arrest

AH-rest

Taking a person into custody, usually for purposes of criminal interrogation and prosecution. Most lawful arrests are performed by the police.

Arson

AR-sun

At common law, burning another's dwelling with knowledge or reckless disregard of the risk. Modern laws expand it to other buildings.

Article I court

AR-tikl wahn kort

A type of U.S. federal court created by Congressional statute. Also called Article I tribunals or legislative courts. They have less independence from the executive branch than Article III courts.

Article III court

AR-tikl three kort

A type of U.S. federal court created under Article III, Section 1 of the U.S. Constitution. The U.S. Supreme Court and U.S. district courts are all examples.

Articles of incorporation

AHR-tih-k'ls uhv in- kor-puh-RAY-shun

A document that creates a corporation. Usually filed with the secretary of state. Lists the name, purpose, and special features of the corporation. Sometimes called certificate of incorporation

Articles of organization

AR-tikls uhv or-gah-niz-AY-shun

The basic charter of a limited liability company (LLC). Similar to the articles of incorporation required to start a corporation. Lists the name, purpose, and financing structure of the LLC. Sometimes called certificates of formation.

Artificial condition

ahr-teh-FIH-shul kuhn-DIH-shun

Something made or put in a certain place by people. Landowners have different responsibilities to warn of dangerous artificial conditions than natural conditions.

Ascertainable

a-sur-TAY'n-ah-b'l

Capable of being verified at some point in time. For example, a will might leave a sum of money to be split between one's children. The actual recipients will only be ascertained when it is time to distribute the money.

Asportation

ass-por-TAY-shun

Physical act of carrying away or removing. Either a person or property may be so moved. A necessary element of crimes such as larceny.

Assault

ah-SAW'lt

An intentional act that puts someone in reasonable apprehension of an imminent battery. Typically, requires more than just words. Emotional fear of harm is not needed; an expectation is enough.

Asset

A-seh't

Something of value that is owned. Assets include cash, bank deposits, rights to receive payment, and even the good will a business builds up in customers' minds.

Assignment

uh-SINE-ment

Transfer of rights to property or to benefits under a contract. This differs from a delegation, which transfers obligations to perform as required by law or contract.

Association

ah-soh-see-EY-shun

(1) A group that is not a separate entity from its individual members; a group that is not a corporation. Usually made for a common purpose.

(2) The sharing of ideas and thoughts between people. The U.S. Constitution's First Amendment protects a right to associate.

Assumption of risk

uh-SUH'mp-shun uhv rih'sk

A defense to negligence that bars recovery if plaintiff accepted the risk of being injured due to defendant's actions. May be expressed or implied.

Attachment

ah-TATCH-ment

(1) In civil procedure, seizure of a person's property to satisfy a judgment against that person. In the typical case, a sheriff seizes property, sells it at auction, and forwards the proceeds to a winning plaintiff.

(2) In secured transactions, the point in time at which a security interest arises in property. A bank's security interest in land attaches when the bank loans money to buy that land as part of a mortgage.

Attempt

ah-TEM'pt

Specific intent to commit a crime, with some overt act towards committing it, but falling short of completing the target crime. Attempt is a crime in itself.

Attorney

uh-TUR-nee

(1) Someone who is specifically authorized by another person to represent the other person in court or in other settings.

(2) More loosely, any lawyer. This includes lawyers who only give private advice and never represent someone in court or other interactions.

Attorney-client privilege

uh-TUR-nee KLAI-yent PRIH-vil-ej

A rule of evidence that protects confidential communication between clients and their attorneys. Clients have the right not to reveal the content of such communication, and to prevent anyone else from disclosing it as well.

Attractive nuisance

a-TRAK-tiv NYOO-sen's

A dangerous condition on land where young people can be expected to visit, posing a danger to children because of their failure to appreciate risks.

Authentication

ah-then-tih-KAY-shun

Proof that a piece of evidence is what the presenting party claims it to be. Examples include testimony from someone who saw a contract being signed, or a technician who took an X-ray image.

Authorized agent

aw-tho-RAI'zd

In civil procedure, a person expressly permitted and required to accept complaints and court summonses on behalf of another party. The party represented is often a corporation.

Authorized shares

AW-thor-ai'zd SHAY'rs

The number of shares that a corporation can legally issue. The exact number is set by the articles of incorporation. *Compare with* outstanding shares, treasury stock.

Automatic stay

aw-to-MA-tik stay

A ban on creditors' demands to collect payment, which kicks in as soon as U.S. bankruptcy proceedings are filed. Secured creditors may be given an exception.

Automobile exception

AW-tow-mo-beel ehk-SEP-shun

One exception to the Fourth Amendment's general warrant requirement. Police may search a vehicle without a warrant if they have probable cause to believe it contains contraband or evidence of a crime.

Award

ah-WOR'd

A final decision in a legal dispute. Especially refers to the dollar amount of damages that is given by a jury or arbitrator.

B

Bad debt

bad deh't

A right to receive money that has become worthless or meaningless. The bankruptcy of a borrower with no valuable assets is one reason bad debt may arise.

Bad faith

bad FAY'th

Intentional dishonesty, failure to acknowledge promises, and failure to observe reasonable standards of fair dealing. Many legal rules penalize parties for acting in bad faith.

Bail

BAY'il

Cash or a bond given as security in exchange for a prisoner's release from confinement. If the prisoner later fails appear in court as required, the court takes possession of the cash or other property pledged.

Bail bond

BA'il bah'nd

Money or property pledged as security in exchange for a prisoner's release from confinement. If the prisoner later fails to appear in court as required, the court takes possession of the money or property.

Bailee

bay-LEE

Someone who accepts property from another party (the bailor), and holds it for a period of time for a certain agreed purpose.

Bailor

BAY-lor; BAY-ler

Someone who delivers his or her property to another party, called the bailee. The bailee then holds the property for a period of time for a certain agreed purpose.

Bankruptcy

BANK-ruhp't-see

Legal proceeding that compensates a debtor's creditors as much as possible, and cancels out remaining debts. Compensation occurs by liquidating debtor's assets, or reorganizing all parties' rights to those assets.

Bankruptcy estate

BANK-ruhp't-see eh-STAY't

Sum of all property rights possessed by a debtor at the start of a bankruptcy case. Includes legal and equitable interests. Some property, such as a home, may be exempted.

Bar association

BAH'r ah-soh-see-EY-shun

An organization whose members are lawyers. May be voluntary or mandatory. For example, a state bar association is a mandatory organization from whom license must be secured to practice law in some state.

Basis
BAY-sis
Amount of money invested in property. Initial basis is equal to the cost of buying property. Adjusted basis reflects later improvements or damages.

Batson challenge
BAT-son CHA-len'j
In court, an objection that the opposing party is using a peremptory challenge to discriminate against a potential juror on the basis of sex, race, or ethnicity.

Battery
BA-tuh-ree
Intentional use of force, without lawful justification, that causes injury to someone. The amount of force can be tiny. Foreseeable chain-reaction events that produce an injury count.

Bench trial
BEN'ch TRAI-yul
A trial in which a judge resolves questions of fact, in addition to questions of law. Some parties prefer a legal expert to weigh their factual disputes, especially in civil trials.

Beneficial owner
beh-neh-FIH-shul OWN-ur
Someone with the right to sell or enjoy something even though legal title is in someone else's name. People who buy corporate stock through a broker are usually beneficial owners. *See* record owner.

Beneficiary
beh-neh-FIH-shuh-ree
Someone entitled to a benefit, or benefiting incidentally from some transaction. For example, people for whose benefit someone makes a trust are called trust beneficiaries.

Bequest
bee-KWEST
Transfer of property through a will upon one's death. Usually refers only to personal property other than money. Also the name for property so transferred.

Best evidence rule
best EH-vih-dens rool
A requirement to produce the original document if attempting to prove terms in the document that are material to the case. Exceptions such as good-faith destruction apply.

Beyond a reasonable doubt
bee-YAH'nd uh REE-zah-nuh'bl DAH'oot
So confident that no reasonble doubt can disturb the conclusion. This burden of persuasion generally applies to

all questions of fact in a criminal trial.

Bifurcation
bai-fur-KAY-shun
Division of something into two parts. A bifurcated trial is held in two stages. One stage usually determines guilt or liability; the other sets punishment or damages.

Bigamy
BIH-guh-mee
Marrying someone while having another living spouse. Traditionally, a strict liability crime. At common law, one could be guilty despite reasonable belief that the other spouse was dead.

Bilateral contract
bye-LAT-eh-rahl KAHN-trakt
Legally enforceable agreement based on the exchange of mutual promises. Promising to sell goods in exchange for a promise to pay is one example.

Bill of attainder
bil uhv uh-TAIN-dur
A legislative act that punishes a specific person or group without trial. Article I of the U.S. Constitution prohibits such acts.

Bill of Rights
bil uhv ruy'ts
A section of law that lists individual rights protected from government intrusion. Often refers to the first ten Amendments of the U.S. Constitution.

Binder
BAI-n'der
(1) In insurance law, a document giving someone temporary coverage before a full insurance agreement is ready.
(2) In real property, a document showing the common intention of seller and buyer to complete the transfer of land. May be accompanied by the buyer's first payment.

Board of directors
bord uhv dih-REK-tors
Governing body of a corporation. After being elected by shareholders, directors establish overarching objectives and appoint executive officers such as CEOs.

Bona fide
BOH-nah FAI'd;   BOH-nah FEE-dee
"In good faith." Refers to good-faith actors or actions that were done in good faith. Also refers to products that are genuinely made as advertised or claimed.

Bona fide purchaser
BOH-nah FAH'id PUR-chah-sur;   BOH-nah FEE-dee PUR-chah-sur
Someone who buys property in good faith, and without actual or constructive notice that the seller may not have

valid title. Also called good-faith purchaser for value.

Bond
BAH'nd
(1) A document promising repayment of a long-term, interest-bearing loan. Both corporations and governments may issue bonds as a way to raise cash. For creditors, secured bonds provide the best assurance of repayment.
(2) In criminal law, a bail bond. Money or property pledged as security in exchange for a prisoner's release from confinement. If the prisoner later fails to appear in court as required, the court takes possession of the money or property.
(3) Loosely, any promise or obligation.

Breach
BREE'ch
A violation of law or contract. Breach of contract involves the failure to perform duties as agreed, or interfering with another party's ability to perform.

Breaking and entering
BRAY-king and EN-teh-ring
At least minimal physical force to gain unlawful entry (breaking), and insertion of any body part or connected object into the building (entering).

Bribe
braib
Unlawful value given in exchange for official action. Both the giver and receiver can be guilty of bribery. The value given is usually money.

Brief
breef
A party's document in court that seeks to prove its position legally correct. Applies relevant legal rules and precedents to the current facts of the dispute.

Broker
BRO-kur
A type of agent that negotiates and closes deals between buyers and sellers. Brokers may deal in securities, insurance, commerce, or trade.

Burden of persuasion
BUR-den uhv pur-SWAY-zhun
The degree of confidence by which someone must prove a position. Also called standard of proof. In criminal cases, "beyond a reasonable doubt" is required. In civil cases, "by a preponderance" is usually enough.

Burden of production
BUR-den uhv prah-DUHK-shun
A party's duty to present enough evidence on some issue so that it can be considered. Without sufficient evidence, a conclusion different from what the party claims will usually stand by default.

Burden of proof

BUR-den uhv proo'f

(1) A party's duty to prove a position in some dispute, or else have the opposite position stand by default. Includes the burden of production and the burden of persuasion.

(2) Sometimes, loosely used as a synonym for the burden of persuasion only.

Burford abstention
BUR-fur'd ab-STEHN-shun

A way for U.S. federal courts to decline cases if resolving them in federal court would interfere with a state's handling of a complex regulatory scheme under its laws.

Burglary
BUR-glah-ree

Breaking and entering into another person's dwelling at night. Requires an intent to commit a felony inside. Many states have dropped the night-time requirement.

Business deductions
BIZ-ness dee-DUK-shuns

Amount of someone's money that is used to earn a living. In the U.S. federal tax code, it can be deducted from taxable income if used to pay for the ordinary and necessary expenses of a job.

Business judgment rule
BIZ-ness JUH'j-ment

A presumption that directors and officers meet their duty of care when they make business decisions. A challenger seeking to prove otherwise must find clear evidence to the contrary.

But-for test
buht for test

The most common test to prove actual causation. It asks whether a result would have occurred if some fact did not exist. If the answer is no, actual causation exists.

Bylaws
BAI-lawz

Written rules that define how a corporation will be run. Prescribes shareholder meetings, describes how directors are elected, and imposes duties on officers.

Bystander
BAI-stan-dur

Someone physically present at a place where something happens, without being directly involved. Bystanders may be highly reliable witnesses if they have no motive to lie.

C

Cafeteria plan
keh-fee-TEE-ree-ah plan
A type of employee benefit plan in the U.S. It lets pre-tax wages go directly into paying for benefits such as health insurance or a flexible spending plan.

Call option
kaw'l AH'p-shun
A contract that allows one party to buy something from another party for a fixed price within a certain time. Used in trading to hedge against price spikes.

Cancellation
KAN-sel-ay-shun
The termination of a promise or contract. Cancellation may occur by express conduct, or by operation of law. The cancelling party may be liable for damages.

Capacity
kah-PA-see-ti
Legal power to enter a transaction or dictate certain results. Typical elements are age (e.g., at least 18 years old) and sound mind. Often refers to the power to create a will or binding contract.

Capital gains
KA-pit'ahl GAY'nz
Profits from anything that is owned to make money (rather than owned for personal use). Includes profit from stocks, bonds, and real estate.

Case-or-controversy requirement
kaes or KAHN-truh-vursie ree-KWA-yer-ment
A rule preventing U.S. federal courts from deciding hypothetical issues. A true case or controversy requires a determination of law in an actual dispute between parties.

Cash method
kash MEH-thud
Accounting method that recognizes income when payment is received. Expenses are not recognized until paid. Most people and businesses use the cash method when paying taxes.

Caucus
KAW-kuh's
A meeting held to create a strategy. Also the act of holding such a meeting. Legislators hold such meetings, as well as mediators when they speak privately with each party in a dispute.

Causa mortis
KAW-za MOR-tis

Caused by contemplation of one's imminent death. A gift *causa mortis* is revocable if the grantor actually lives through whatever might have caused death.

Cause
kawz

Some force or reason that leads to a result. Causes may be singular or joint; predictable or unforeseen. *See, e.g.,* actual cause, proximate cause.

Cause of action
AK-shun

Set of facts that entitles one to a remedy in court. The elements required for a certain cause of action (e.g., battery) are defined by statutes and past court decisions.

Caveat
KAH-vee-aht

(1) A statement of caution or warning. For example, a legal rule might include a caveat whereby one acting in bad faith will be treated differently than everyone else.

(2) Formal notice given to a court that requests a pause in proceedings. The typical reason is that proceedings are currently ignoring someone's interests without proper hearing.

Caveat emptor
KAH-vee-aht EMP-tor

"Buyer beware." A rule that leaves buyers few rights to complain about defects in property after buying it. Modified by modern statutes and case law.

Certification
sur-teh-fih-KAY-shun

(1) The act of confirming something as valid. Also the name for a statement attesting to validity. For example, official driving records should be certified by the Department of Motor Vehicles.

(2) A way for courts to ask for guidance from more authoritative courts on questions of law. Federal appeals courts may present questions for review to the U.S. Supreme Court or the highest court of any state.

Challenge
CHA-len'j

(1) An attack on someone's legal qualifications. One example is filing suit to see if the president is a natural-born citizen of the country.

(2) In court, a party's request to dismiss someone from a jury panel. *See* challenge for cause, peremptory challenge.

Challenge for cause
CHA-len'j for kawz

A party's request to dismiss someone from a jury panel, when that request is supported by a valid reason. Reasons include bias or prejudice.

Chapter 11
CHAP-tur ee-LEH-ven

The part of U.S. bankruptcy law used when seeking to reorganize the rights of debtors and creditors in the debtor's assets. Used mostly by debtor corporations.

Chapter 13

CHAP-tur thir-TEEN

The part of U.S. bankruptcy law used when seeking to reorganize the rights of debtors and creditors in an individual debtor's assets. Cannot be used by debtor corporations.

Chapter 7

CHAP-tur SEH-ven

The part of U.S. bankruptcy law used when seeking to liquidate (sell off) a debtor's assets for the benefit of creditors. Used by debtor individuals and corporations.

Character evidence

KA-rak-ter EH-vih-dens

Opinion or facts about someone's morality or general psychological traits. In general, not admissible in civil trials, nor in criminal trials if first raised by the prosecution.

Charitable trust

CHE-rih-tah-b'l truh'st

A trust created with some goal of giving social help or advancing ideas. A charitable trust usually has many beneficiaries over time. The rule against perpetuities does not apply to these trusts.

Charter

CHAH'r-ter

A document that creates a regional government or business organization. Articles of incorporation are a type of charter that creates corporations.

Chattel

CHA-t'l

All movable property and rights to intangible property such as patents. Also called personal property.

Child support

chai'ild suh-PORT

A legal duty by parents to contribute financially to the needs of their children. Such needs include basic necessities and education. The duty continues until children reach the age of majority, complete secondary schooling, or obtain emancipation.

Circumstantial

SUR-kum-stan-shul

Indirect and incapable of proving something without logical inferences or guesses. For example, a lifeless body can be circumstantial proof that someone was killed.

Citizenship

SIHT-eh-zen-ship

Membership and allegiance to a certain government or governments. For jurisdiction purposes, people are citizens of the state where domiciled. Corporations are citizens of the state where incorporated and the state with their principal place of business.

Claim

KLAY'm

(1) Some right, property interest, or set of facts that entitles one to a remedy in court. Often used synonymously with cause of action.

(2) More loosely, any argument, or demand for something such as money. Such claims may be right or wrong, and lawful or unlawful.

Claim preclusion

KLAY'm pree-KLYOO-zhun

A rule that prohibits parties from re-filing or contesting claims that have been fully decided in court on their merits. Unlike collateral estoppel, applies to an entire cause of action and not just a single issue.

Class action

klas AK-shun

A type of case with one individual plaintiff (or a small group of people) representing the interests of a large group. The actual plaintiffs must share interests with people in the group, and represent those interests sufficiently well.

Client trust account

KLAI-yent truh'st UH-kount

A bank account created to hold legal fees and expenses paid in advance by a client. A lawyer may withdraw funds from such account as they are earned.

Client-lawyer relationship

KLAI-yent LOH-yer

Formal relationship between a client and lawyer, giving rights and duties to each party. Arises by mutual agreement, by court order, or by a lawyer's failure to refuse representation after knowing that the prospective client is relying on the lawyer to provide services.

Close corporation

KLOH's kor-puh-RAY-shun

A corporation without publicly traded shares. Instead, all shares in the corporation are owned by a few shareholders (often family members). Sometimes called private corporation.

Code

KO'(u)d

A collection of current laws organized by topic. Almost every jurisdiction publishes a code. It can also be a proposed set of laws to organize the rules on a subject.

Codicil

KO-dih-sil

A document that supplements or changes the terms of a will. To be valid, its execution must meet the same requirements as a will.

Collateral

kah-LEH-teh-rahl

(1) Property in which someone has a security interest. In the typical case, an owner keeps possession of the collateral. But if a loan is not repaid, a creditor may take and resell the collateral to satisfy a debt.

(2) A descriptive term for anything that is secondary or on the side. For example, in civil procedure, a collateral attack is a new case that challenges findings from an earlier case.

Collateral attack

kah-LEH-teh-rahl AH-tak

A new challenge to a judgment from an earlier case. This differs from a direct appeal because it is no longer part of a direct route with time limitations at every step. Habeas corpus proceedings are one example.

Collateral estoppel

kah-LEH-teh-rahl eh-STAH'pl

A rule that prohibits parties from contesting issues that were already decided in court as part of a final judgment. Also called issue preclusion.

Collateral order exception

kah-LEH-teh-rahl OR-der

One way to appeal from a court's interlocutory order. The order must completely resolve an issue that is separate from the cause of action. It must also concern an important right that could be irreperably lost without immediate appellate review.

Collateral source rule

kah-LEH-teh-rahl sors rool

A prohibition on the decrease of awarded tort damages simply because an indepedent source (e.g., insurance) gave the plaintiff some compensation.

Collision coverage

kuh-LIH-zhun KAH-ver-ej

Insurance that covers damage to the insured party's automobile from contact with other objects. It does not cover any resulting personal injuries.

Color of law

KUH-lur uhv law

An appearance or perception that some action or threatened action is supported by legal rules. The term is often used in hindsight when it is clear that the action was unlawful.

***Colorado River* abstention**

kah-lah-RAH-dow RIH-vur ab-STEHN-shun

A way for U.S. federal courts to decline cases if the parties are attempting to run simultaneous state and federal cases on the same legal issues.

Commerce Clause

KAH-murs klawz

Article I, Section 8, Clause 3 of the U.S. Constitution. It gives Congress exclusive power to regulate commerce across U.S. state lines and with other nations.

Commercial speech
kah-MER-shul spee-ch

The type of expression found in advertising and business communications. The U.S. Constitution's First Amendment only gives some protection to commercial speech that is truthful.

Commingled
koh-MIN-guld

Mixed or put together. For example, commingled funds are different sources of money moved into a single account. Commingling can make it hard to determine proper ownership.

Common law
KAH-mun

Rules that come from past court decisions, as opposed to legislative statutes and constitutions. U.S. legal culture came mostly from the English common law.

Common stock
KAH-mun STAH'k

A type of ownership share in a corporation that comes with voting rights. In the case of liquidation, common stockholders get paid last - and only if assets remain after creditors and preferred stockholders are paid.

Comparative negligence
kuhm-PA-ra-tiv NEG-le-jens

A defense to negligence that lowers plaintiff's recovery in proportion to plaintiff's own negligence. A partial version of this defense cuts off all recovery if plaintiff was more than 50% at fault for the accident.

Competent
KAH'm-peh-tent

(1) Having the knowledge, skill, and level of preparation needed for some activity. Professional service providers (such as lawyers) have a duty of competence to their clients.

(2) Evidence that does not violate any rule of exclusion. Incompetent evidence is inadmissible. For example, evidence can be incompetent if it is hearsay, subject to a privilege, or unconstitutionally obtained.

Complaint
kahm-PLAINT

A pleading that begins a civil or criminal case. It explains the court's jurisdiction, asks for judicial relief, and outlines the civil claim or criminal charge.

Compounding a crime
kahm-PAH'oon-ding a craim

Accepting value in exchange for hiding a crime, or agreeing not to prosecute it. The value involved is usually money.

Concurrent estate

KAHN-kur'ent eh-STAY't

Ownership in certain property that is held by multiple people at the same time. Examples include joint tenancy, tenancy by the entirety, and tenancy in common.

Condemnation

kahn-dem-NAY-shun

(1) A government's decision that certain private property must go to public use. Reasons include public safety and economic revitalization. Also called eminent domain.

(2) A declaration that someone is guilty of something. To be official, must come from a court. Loosely, can be anyone's expression of opinion.

Condition

kuhn-DIH-shun

A fact or event whose existence or non-existence will have an effect on something else. Many legal rules and contracts include conditions for determining results.

Condition precedent

kuhn-DIH-shun preh-SEE-dent

A specified fact or event that must exist or happen before a contractual duty becomes due. If the condition never happens, the party is released from its duty and no breach occurs.

Condition subsequent

kuhn-DIH-shun sub-SEH-kwent

A specified fact or event whose occurrence will cancel something or bring it to an end. That something is often a contractual duty or property estate.

Confidentiality

kahn-fih-den-shee-A-lee-tee

Secrecy. Information that is legally deemed confidential cannot be shared without consent of the person for whom the protection exists.

Confirmation

kahn-fur-MAY-shun

Approval. In bankruptcy law, refers to the court's approval for a plan of reorganization in debtor's assets.

Confirmation bias

kahn-fur-MAY-shun BAH-yus

A tendency to favor information that supports one's theory or gut feeling on an issue. Also called biased assimilation.

Conflict of interest

KAHN-flik't uhv INT-rest

An actual or reasonably expected contradiction between the interests of two parties, or between the dual roles of one person. A police officer on duty has a conflict of interest when he sees his wife speeding.

Conflict of laws

KAHN-flik't uhv lawz

The area of law concerned with deciding cases where the laws of different jurisdictions might be reasonably applied.

Confrontation right

kon-fron-TAY-shun ruy't

A criminal defendant's right to confront an accuser in court and check the testimony of that witness through cross-examination. The U.S. Constitution's Sixth Amendment protects the right of confrontation.

Consent

KAHN-sent

Voluntary agreement that something be done. Valid consent to tortious behavior precludes damages for the tort. Valid consent to a warrantless search precludes suppression of the evidence at trial.

Consequential damages

kuhn-seh-KWEN-shul DAM-eh-jes

Losses that do not flow automatically from an injury, but instead happen indirectly to the injured party because of special circumstances. Also called special damages.

Consideration

KUHN-sih-de-ray-shun

A bargained-for exchange involving something of legal value. To have legal value, the promised item or action must be a benefit to someone, or a detriment to someone else. Every contract needs consideration or a valid substitute.

Consignment

kuhn-SAI'n-ment

Delivery of goods by an owner to another party (typically a merchant). The other party attemps to sell or otherwise transfer the goods on the owner's behalf.

Consolidation

kon-sah-lih-DAY-shun

In general, the combination of multiple things into a new one. In specific contexts:

(1) Dissolution of two business organizations, and the creation of a new one that accepts liabilities and assets of the dissolved ones. Corporations are the usual businesses involved.
(2) Unification of multiple court cases into one. Courts usually order consolidation when multiple cases involve the same parties, events, and disputes.

Conspiracy

KAHN-spee-rah-see

Intentional agreement between two or more people to commit a crime, with a specific intent to have it completed. Most states also require an overt act towards committing the crime.

Constitution

kahn-sti-TYU-shun

Fundamental legal setup for a state or country. Defines the government, official institutions, and personal rights. Often exists in written form.

Construction
kuhn-STRUH'k-shun

The process of determining how something should be interpreted. Most often, refers to a court's interpretation of a contract, statute, or constitution.

Constructive
kun-STRUH'k-tiv

Legally recognized despite not actually happening or existing. For example, constructive delivery occurs if something is given and the receiving party manifests consent but forgets to pick up the item.

Constructive trust
kun-STRUH'k-tiv truh'st

A trust imposed on the owner of property by a court. For example, a defendant who stole property may become a constructive trustee, with plaintiffs as beneficiaries. Also called involuntary trust.

Contempt
KUN-tem-p't

In general, a state of events in which someone is despised. In court or a legislature, an official announcement that a witness, lawyer, or someone else has disrespected the authority of the institution. Someone held in contempt may be punished by imprisonment or a fine.

Contingent
KAHN-tin-jent

Uncertain or subject to a condition. For example, a future property interest in a person's children is contingent on that person having children.

Contingent fee
kahn-TIN-jent fee

Legal fee that depends on the outcome of a matter. Lawyers are generally prohibited from agreeing to contingent fees from criminal defendants and parties to domestic relations disputes.

Contract
KAHN-trakt

An agreement between two or more parties that creates legally enforceable obligations. Unperformed obligations can make a party liable for damages.

Contract Clause
KAHN-trakt klawz

Article I, Section 10, Clause 1 of the U.S. Constitution. It strongly limits the power of states to pass laws that retroactively change contractual obligations.

Contract of adhesion
KAHN-trakt uhv ad-HEE-zhun

A contract drafted by one party and signed by another with little choice but to accept the terms. Sometimes unenforceable due to unconscionability. Also called a standard form contract.

Contribution
kahn-trih-BYOO-shun
The right of a co-debtor who overpaid his share to demand reimbursement from other co-debtors. The debtors usually owe money because they lost a case as joint defendants.

Contributory negligence
kahn-TRIH-byoo-to-ree NEG-le-jens
A defense to negligence that bars recovery if the plaintiff was also negligent. Leads to harsh outcomes for many plaintiffs. Replaced by comparative negligence in majority of U.S. states.

Conversion
KUHN-vur-zhun
Intentional act that infringes on one's right to possess his or her personal property. Unlike trespass to chattels, serious enough to order full payment for the item's value.

Conveyance
kahn-VEH-yuns
Voluntary transfer of property rights from one living person to another. For example, a contract to sell land followed by a deed delivery is a conveyance.

Copyright
kah-pee-RUY't
Exclusive right to copy, distribute, and otherwise profit from a work of authorship. Includes books, music, theatrical plays, paintings, and movies.

Corporation
kor-puh-RAY-shun
A legal organization with rights to act as a single person distinct from its owners, managers, and employees. Most corporations are made for business purposes.

Corpus
KOR-pus
Body. For example, the property placed in a trust for management by the trustee is called a corpus. Such property can also be called a res. It differs from trust income, which is money earned by investing the corpus.

Corpus delicti
KOR-pus de-LIK-tee; KOR-pus de-LIK-tai
"Body of the crime." The behavior involved in a crime, and the physical objects upon which the crime was committed. For example, a dead body.

Corroborating evidence
kah-RAH-buh-ray-ting EH-vih-dens
Facts that strengthen or confirm whatever version of events is suggested by previously heard or discovered evidence.

Counterclaim

KAH'oon-ter-klay'm

A claim filed by the defendant against the plaintiff. May be unrelated to plaintiff's claims. If mandatory, counterclaims must be filed or lost. If permissive, may be brought later in a separate case.

Course of dealing

koh'rs uhv DEE-ling

General norms and expectations that come from previous contracts between two or more parties.

Course of performance

koh'rs uhv pehr-FOR-muns

General norms and expectations that come from past transactions under a single contract.

Court-connected mediation

kort kah-NEHK-ted mee-dee-A-shun

Mediation that starts by suggestion or order from a judge in ongoing court litigation. A major goal is cutting costs, although failed mediation can appear wasteful in hindsight.

Covenant

KUH-veh-nant

Formal promise expressed as part of a contract. Used interchangeably with the word "promise," but has a more solemn and ceremonial connotation.

Credit

KREH-dit

(1) Process of borrowing money for later repayment. Also, the name for faith that money will be repaid.

(2) Increase in revenues, or a decrease in money owed. The opposite of debit in accounting.

(3) Belief in something, or the act of believing something. A jury that accepts the testimony of a witness may be said to credit that testimony.

Creditor

KREH-dih-tor

Someone with legal right to expect repayment of a debt. Lending banks are creditors. Plaintiffs awarded money damages are called judgment creditors.

Crime

craim

An act that is deemed a wrongful offense against the public, and punished by the government. The common law used to define many crimes. Today, almost all crimes are defined by legislatures.

Criminal negligence

KRIH-mih-nul NEG-le-jens

An act of gross negligence so extreme or blameworthy that it may be punished as a crime.

Cross-claim

kros KLAY'm

A claim by one party against a co-party. For example, if a bank and insurance company are both defendants in a case, a claim by one against the other is a cross-claim.

Cross-examination

kros eg-zam-ih-NAY-shun

Set of questions posed to a witness after the end of direct examination at trial. Asked by the party who opposes the party that called up the witness.

Cruel and unusual punishment

krool and ahn-YOO-zhoo-ahl PUH-nish-ment

Punishment that is grossly disproportionate to the crime, amounts to torture, or otherwise schocks the conscience. Prohibited by the U.S. Constitution's Eighth Amendment.

Curtilage

KUR-teh-lej

The land and yard next to one's dwelling. The exact size and extent of curtilage varies. Questions to ask include whether a fence surrounds the area and how the area is used.

Custodial interrogation

kah-STOH-dee-al in-te-rah-GAY-shun

Involuntary detention by the police ("custody"), during which the police ask anything that is reasonably likely to spur incriminating statements by the person detained ("interrogation").

D

Damages

DAM-eh-jes

Money that is requested or ordered to be paid as compensation for an injury. *See, e.g.*, general damages, consequential damages, punitive damages.

Data mining

DAY-tah MAI-ning

Analysis of data for patterns. May be used in police surveillance to catch suspicious activity. For example, credit card records may be searched to find buyers of explosive materials and electrical wires.

De facto

dee FAK-tow

Having actual existence even though not conforming to legal requirements. Thus, someone might be de facto president despite unlawfully taking power.

De jure

dey ZHU-ree; de YOO-ree

"By law." Refers to something that exists (or should exist) by virtue of legally prescribed rules. One might be a de jure president even if not actually able to exercise power.

De minimis

deh MIN-eh-mis

So small that it may be ignored. For example, *de minimis* benefits that workers gain at work (e.g., occasional personal use of a printer) do not count as income.

De novo

deh NO-vo

"From the beginning." For example, de novo review is an appellate court's fresh examination of a lower body's decision without deference to the lower body's decisions.

Dead man's statute

dehd man's STA'tch-yoot

A law that prevents interested witnesses from testifying in court about discussions or deals with people who are now dead. Does not apply to criminal cases.

Deadly force

DEHD-lee fors

Action that may be reasonably expected to cause death or serious bodily harm. Many defenses fail if the defendant used deadly force.

Debit

DEH-bit

(1) Process of paying money directly out of a bank account.

(2) Increase in money owed, or a decrease in revenues. The opposite of credit in accounting.

Debt
deht

Anything legally owed to someone else by law. Often refers to money, but can also include services or property.

Debtor
DEH-tor

Someone with a legal duty to repay another. Money borrowers are debtors. Defendants who are judged liable for money damages are called judgment debtors.

Decedent
deh-SEE-dent

A person who has died. For courts, one immediate question is whether the decedent left a valid will or not.

Declarant
dek-LA-rant

The person who makes a statement. This word distinguishes a person who made a hearsay statement from the witness who claims to have heard it.

Declaration
dek-lah-RAY-shun

(1) A person's voluntary statement, recorded in writing, but not sworn to or notarized. Despite lack of notarization, declarations promise truthfulness on penalty of perjury.

(2) Loosely, any statement or announcement.

Declaratory judgment
deh-KLA-ra-to-ree JUH'j-ment

A court's ruling that conclusively establishes the rights of different parties in a certain dispute before anyone has suffered actual injury that needs redress.

Decree
deh-KREE

(1) Any order from a court, especially one that orders specific action to be taken. Often refers to a court's decision in a family-law case. For example, a divorce decree is the official document granting a divorce.

(2) Historically, the name for a judgment issued by some tribunal that was not a court of law. For example, the decisions of a court of equity would be known as decrees. *See* equity (def. 4).

Deduction
dee-DUK-shun

Reduction or subtraction. In tax codes, deductions may be taken for business expenses, losses, and personal deductions such as charitable gifts.

Deed
dee'd

(1) A written document that officially and finally transfers a property interest. Most often refers to sales of land.

Signed and delivered to the new owner.

(2) In general, any act or action. For example, a convicted criminal may be said to have done bad deeds.

Defamation

deh-fah-MAY-shun

A statement by one person that adversely affects another's reputation when communicated to a third party. Defenses include truth of the statement, and various privileges based on the type of issues and people involved.

Default

deh-FAW'lt

Failure to perform a legal obligation, such as the payment of debt. Courts may issue default judgments against parties that fail to answer complaints or follow orders.

Default judgment

deh-FOLT JUH'j-ment

A judgment entered against a party that fails to make an appearance in court, plead in response to a complaint, respond to orders, or otherwise neglect its duties.

Defeasible fee

deh-FEEZ-uh'bl

Ownership of certain property that may last forever like a fee simple absolute, but that could end if a stated event occurs.

Defective incorporation

de-FEK-tiv in- kor-puh-RAY-shun

The attempted creation of a corporation that fails to meet legal standards. For instance, the articles of incorporation might lack essential elements required for proper filing.

Defendant

deh-FEHN-dent

The party accused of civil or criminal misconduct in a lawsuit. May be a person or entity, such as a corporation or government.

Defense of others

deh-FENS uhv AH-thers

Use of force to protect another person from harm. This defense usually exists whenever one reasonably thinks that the other person would be entitled to use self-defense.

Defense of property

deh-FENS uhv PRAH-per-tee

A defense that may allow one to use force against someone who harms property, or poses an imminent threat to property. Deadly force is not allowed by this defense.

Deferment

deh-FUR-ment

Delay or postponement. Contractual duties, military service, jury duty, and worker compensation may all be deferred with the permission of relevant parties.

Deficiency
de-FIH-shen-see

Less of something than required to fill a need. A house sold in foreclosure for less money than owed in loans and fees may leave the debtor personally liable for the rest.

Delegation
de-le-GAY-shun

Transfer of obligations to perform as required by law or contract. This differs from an assignment, which transfers the rights to receive some benefit.

Deliberate
(1) *de-LIH-beh-rut*

Descriptive term that refers to anything that is intentional. Deliberate action is action that is done voluntarily, usually with a specific goal in mind.

(2) *de-LIH-beh-ray't*

The act of thinking through an issue, especially as a group of people. Juries and legislatures are often said to deliberate when they meet to decide specific questions.

Deliberate and premeditated murder
de-LIH-beh-rut and pre-MEH-dih-tay-ted MUR-der

A murder with two features: the decision to kill was made in a cool state without passion (deliberate), and defendant actually reflected on the idea of killing (premeditated).

Delinquent
deh-lin-KWENT

Wrongful or late. Criminals under 18 years old may be called juvenile delinquents. A missed payment may be called delinquent debt.

Delivery
deh-LIH-ve-ree

Formal transfer of property, or rights to its possession. The property (or document proving rights) need not always be put in physical possession of the recipient. Constructive delivery is often enough.

Demurrer
deh-MYOO-rer

A pleading in court, arguing that even if plaintiff's allegations are true, no valid cause of action has been presented. Now called a motion to dismiss (for failure to state a claim) in most U.S. jurisdictions.

Deposition
deh-pah-ZIH-shun

Setting in which a witness testifies out of court ahead of a possible trial. Any party may attend and ask questions, often through an attorney.

Depreciation
dee-pree-she-A-shun

Gradual decrease in the value of property. In tax law, depreciation is the process for gradually subtracting the cost of income-generating property from income over the useful life of the property.

Derivative claim
de-RI-vah-tiv KLAY'm
A shareholder's lawsuit filed on behalf of the corporation. Typically accuses directors and officers of violating their duties to the corporation. Any damages awarded go to the corporation.

Derivative work
deh-RIH-vah-tiv work
A document or other expression that includes significant copyrighted elements from earlier works. Derivative works must show sufficient originality to be copyrighted.

Derivatives
de-RI-vah-tivs
Financial notes whose value depends on the underlying value of something else. The underlying value is usually the price of a traded stock or commodity. Can be used as insurance or as risky speculation.

Design defect
deh-ZAIN DEE-fekt
A problem with the concept or blueprint for an item. Unlike manufacturing defects, affects all items of the same product line. Includes dangerous parts and packaging.

Design patent
deh-ZAI'n PAT'nt
A type of patent issued for a newly invented and ornamental design. Can come from any field, such as electronics, furniture, and jewelry.

Destination contract
des-tih-NAY-shun KAHN-trakt
A deal in which the seller is responsible for risk of loss or damage to goods until they arrive at the destination specified by contract. *Compare with* shipment contract.

Detention
dee-TEN-shun
Confinement or delay of a person. Police detentions count as seizures, and must comply with the Fourth Amendment. Detention occurs whenever a reasonable person would not believe that he or she is free to leave.

Deterrence
deh-TUR-ens
Prevention of certain behavior. Deterrence of harmful and offensive acts is an important goal behind criminal laws.

Devise
deh-VAIZ
Transfer of real property through a will upon one's death. Also the name for real property so transferred. *See* bequest, legacy.

Dicta

DIK-tah

Short version of *obiter dictum* ("said by the way"). Statements made in a judicial opinion that do not set a precedent because they are not essential to the holding. Dictum is a single statement of this kind.

Direct

DIH-rekt

(1) Connected without interference. For example, direct evidence in a trial relates to some material issue without the need for any logical inferences or guesses.

(2) To guide or instruct. For example, a judge who sets deadlines for a case may be said to direct how the case proceeds.

Direct claim

dih-REK't KLAY'm

A shareholder's lawsuit filed on behalf of him or herself. It claims wrongful deprivation of the shareholder's personal rights as an owner of the corporation.

Direct examination

dih-REK't eg-zam-ih-NAY-shun

First set of questions posed to a witness testifying at trial. Asked by the party who called the witness to testify.

Directed verdict

dih-REK-ted VER-dee'kt

A judge's order to a jury, compelling it to decide an issue in a certain way because no legally sufficient reason exists for another conclusion.

Director

dih-REK-tor

Loosely, anyone who acts as a chief administrator. In a corporation, someone elected or appointed to the highest level of government within a corporation.

Disbursement

dis-BURS-ment

The act of paying. Typically, payment is made from an existing fund of money in response to proof that payment is owed.

Disclaimer

dis-CLAY-mur

The renunciation of a legal right or burden. Sellers may disclaim warranties, testators may disclaim their wills, and prize winners may disclaim their prizes.

Disclosure

dis-KLOH-zhur

Revelation of something not previously known or available to others. In federal civil procedure, parties must immediately disclose minimum information (e.g., witness names) without waiting for a discovery request.

Discovery

dis-KAH-veh-ree

Process by which parties to a case locate evidence that is related to the dispute. May include depositions, interrogatories, requests for production, and other tools.

Discretionary jurisdiction

dis-KREH-shun-ary joo-ris-DIK-shun

A court's power to decide if it wishes to hear a case. A court with such power may decline a case even if it has jurisdiction over the subject-matter and parties.

Discretionary trust

dis-KREH-shuh-na-ree truh'st

A protective trust in which the trustee often has full discretion to decide if, when, and in what amount payments should be made. Sometimes, guidelines exist for the trustee to consult.

Discrimination

dis-cri-mi-NAY-shun

The result of laws that give or deny privileges to certain groups of people. Some types of discrimination are lawful while others are not.

Dismissal

dis-MIH-suhl

Official termination of a case. Complaints without merit, ignored orders, and voluntary settlements between the parties may all lead to cases being dismissed.

Dissociation

dih-SOH-see-ey-shun

A partner's withdrawal from a partnership. May result by voluntary decision of the partner, expulsion by the other partners, or because of the partner's bankruptcy.

Dissolution

dih-suh-LYOO-shun

The termination of a previously existing legal arrangement (often a corporation or partnership). Bankruptcy, expiration of time, or a voluntary decision may all be the cause of dissolution.

Diversity jurisdiction

dai-VUR-seh-tee joo-ris-DIK-shun

The power of U.S. federal courts to hear disputes involving diversity of citizenship and a minimum amount in controversy (e.g., $75,000). No single party from one side can be a citizen of the same state as any party on another.

Dividend

DIH-vih-dend

Part of a corporation's earnings or profits, which may be distributed amongst shareholders. May consist of cash or additional shares. Corporations are not generally required to issue dividends.

Doctrine of worthier title

DAHK-trin uhv WOR-thee-er TAH'i-tl

A property law rule that converts a remainder in grantor's heirs into a reversion for the grantor. Sometimes rebuttable, so that grantor's devisees under a will may lose the property to grantor's heirs.

Domestic authority

dah-MES-tik uh-THO-reh-tee

The right to use nondeadly and reasonble force when legally caring for someone. May be used as a defense in court. One example is discipline of children.

Domicile

DAH-mih-sah-il

A person's true home; the place they intend to return if ever away. In U.S. courts, the state of one's domicile determines one's citizenship.

Dominion

DAH-meen'yun

Complete control over something. When paying taxes, money is not added to income unless the taxpayer has full dominion over that money.

Dormant Commerce Clause

DOHR-ment KAH-murs klawz

A rule inferred from the Commerce Clause. It generally prevents states from regulating interstate commerce even if Congress has not passed conflicting laws.

Double jeopardy

DUH'bl JE-par-dee

General prohibition on holding a second trial for the same alleged crime. Still, exceptions exist for events such as a hung jury, mistrial for clear necessity, some retrials of defendants who win their appeals.

Duces tecum

DYOO-ses TEE-kuhm

"Bring with you." For example, a subpoena *duces tecum* orders the recipient to appear somewhere, and to bring certain documents along.

Due diligence

dyoo DIH-lih-jens

An amount of effort that is sufficiently reasonable for a given situation. For example, a lawyer's due diligence when handling a financial case might include obtaining help from an accountant.

Due process

dyu PRAH-ses

Set of legal rules designed to protect individual rights. The U.S. Constitution's Fifth and Fourteenth Amendments protect due process, along with various state laws. *See* substantive due process, procedural due process.

DUI

dee yoo ai

Driving under the influence of alcohol or other drugs. Usually a misdemeanor offense. May be a felony if serious injury results.

DUII

dee yoo ai ai

Driving under the influence of intoxicants, or driving under intense influence. Refers to alcohol or other drugs. Usually a misdemeanor offense. May be a felony if serious injury results.

Durable power of attorney

DYOO-rah-b'l PAU-er uhv uh-TUR-nee

A document in which one designates an agent to act and make decisions in his or her place, even in the event of incapacitation or disability.

Duress

dyoo-RES

Harm that is threatened to force a person to sign a contract or do anything else against his will. In the extreme case, may include physical confinement and actual harm.

***Durham* test**

DUR-em test

Insanity defense requiring that defendant would not have committed the crime but for a mental illness or defect. Also known as the New Hampshire test.

Duty

DYU-tee

A legal obligation. Duties may be imposed by law or contract. Affirmative duties are duties to do something. Negative duties are duties not to do something.

Duty of care

DYU-tee uhv KAY'r

A duty to work diligently, including staying informed and carefully examining business proposals. Directors, officers, partners, members, managers, and agents all have a duty of care to their business organizations or principals.

Duty of loyalty

DYU-tee uhv LO-yal-tee

A duty to work impartially on behalf of one's business, and to avoid implicating one's personal interests. Directors, officers, partners, members, managers, and agents all have a duty of loyalty to their business organizations or principals.

Duty of obedience

DYU-tee uhv oh-BEE-dee-ens

An agent's duty to act within his or her actual authority, and to follow any reasonable directions of the principal.

Duty to account

DYU-tee too UH-kount

An agent's duty to reimburse the principal for any liability stemming from the agent's misconduct. Relevant misconduct includes violating the duties of care, loyalty, and obedience.

Duty to indemnify

DYU-tee too in-DEM-ni-fai

A principal's duty to reimburse the agent for the costs of representation. Payments that further a principal's interests are an example of such costs.

Duty to mitigate

DYU-tee too MIH-tee-gayt

A party's duty to minimize damages resulting from the other party's breach of contract. Thus, an improperly fired employee has a duty to diligently look for replacement work.

DWI

dee dah-b'l-yoo ai

Driving while intoxicated by alcohol or other drugs. Usually a misdemeanor offense. May be a felony if serious injury results.

E

Easement

EEZ-ment

A limited right to use land that is owned by someone else. For example, a farmer could sell an easement letting someone place a billboard on the farm.

Effective assistance of counsel

eh-FEK-tiv uh-SIS-tens uhv KAUN-sel

Meaningful and careful legal representation. The U.S. Constitution's Sixth Amendment protects a criminal defendant's right to such representation.

Elective share

ee-LEK-tiv SHAY'r

The right of a spouse or child to take a minimum share of an estate if granted an insufficient inheritance under the will. The right comes from various state statutes.

Embezzlement

em-BEZ'l-ment

Fraudulent taking of property after being entrusted to handle it by someone in lawful possession. A cashier stealing from the register is one example.

Employee

em-PLOH-yee

Someone who works for another party under some express or implied hiring agreement. The other party (employer) controls the manner in which work is done.

Employer

em-PLOH-yer

A person or business that hires someone to perform work. Work is done under an express or implied hiring agreement, and the employer controls the details of the work.

Enjoin

en-JOY'n

To impose an injunction, or to otherwise order or prohibit certain action. For example, a court forcing parties to perform under their contract may be said to enjoin them.

Enterprise liability

EN-ter-praiz lah-yah-BIH-leh-tee

Liability imposed on a business. Businesses may be held criminally liable. They may also be held liable in tort, as when personal injury victims win a judgment against all the manufacturers who contributed to the injury.

Entrapment

en-TRAP-ment

Inducement or persuasion to commit a crime, done by law enforcement officials, in hopes of then arresting the target. Entrapment is a defense in criminal cases.

Equal protection
EE-kwahl pruh-TEK-shun
A requirement that laws must generally treat similarly situated persons in the same way. Discriminatory laws may be invalid depending on the discriminatory classification at stake. The U.S. Constitution's Fourteenth Amendment requires equal protection of the laws.

Equitable servitude
EH-kwi-tuh'bl SUR-vih-tyood
A promise to do or not do something with one's land. Enforceable in court through equitable remedies such as injunctions and specific performance, rather than money damages.

Equity
EH-kwi-tee
(1) Justice or fairness.
(2) A share of ownership in property. Money raised from selling stock in a business is often called equity finance.
(3) General name for many judicial remedies other than money damages. Examples include injunctions and specific performance. They are called equitable remedies.
(4) Court of equity. In the past, many courts of equity existed that only heard cases that properly called for equitable remedies. These cases were called "suits in equity," and stood in contrast to "actions at law." This distinction was abandoned in most U.S. jurisdictions.

Erie doctrine
EE-ree DAHK-trin
A rule for deciding conflicts between U.S. state and federal laws when hearing a case based on diversity of citizenship. In general, state law prevails unless the U.S. Constitution, federal statute, or a federal rule of evidence or procedure applies.

Escheat
is-CHEET
A rule giving ownership of property to the state after its owner dies without a will and without any heirs. Also the name for property so transferred.

Estate
eh-STAY't
The degree and nature of someone's interest in property. For example, one might have unrestricted ownership (fee simple absolute), or ownership until death (life estate).

Estoppel
eh-STAH'pl
General legal principle that prohibits fundamentally unfair action. For example, one may be prohibited by estoppel from contradicting one's earlier claim. *See also* promissory estoppel, collateral estoppel.

Eviction

eh-VIK-shun

A legal process to take possession away from tenants who may have lawfully occupied property in the past.

Ex parte
eks PAHR-tey

Coming from one side or party only. Refers to communication or action taken without giving a competing party notice or opportunity to respond.

Ex post facto
eks poast FAK-toh

Having retroactive effect. Ex post facto laws apply retroactively, so that an action legal when done may be declared illegal and prosecuted. The U.S. Constitution prohibits ex post facto laws.

Exception
ehk-SEP-shun

A decision that although something falls into a category, it should be disregarded or not have the same effect. Most legal rules have exceptions for special circumstances.

Excise tax
EHK-size

A tax on products made or sold domestically in a country. For example, an excise tax might be placed on soda drinks to fund diabetes research.

Exclusion
eks-KLYOO-zhun

A decision not to include something in a category. Thus, exclusions from income are not added to gross income. Excluded evidence is not heard by a jury.

Exclusionary rule
eks-KLYOO-zhah-neh-ree rool

In criminal trials, a prohibition on using evidence that was obtained in violation of the defendant's rights under the Fourth, Fifth, or Sixth Amendments.

Exclusive jurisdiction
eks-KLYU-siv joo-ris-DIK-shun

A court's power to hear at least one type of case that no other court can hear. Thus, a state may send all tax disputes to a specially created tax court.

Exculpatory evidence
eks-KUL-pah-to-ree EH-vih-dens

Evidence that tends to prove someone's innocence of a crime. In a criminal trial, prosecutors must disclose such evidence given a reasonable probability that it would affect the verdict or sentencing.

Excuse
eks-KYOO'z

A defense that relieves people from blame, but only because an independent factor forced them to commit otherwise wrongful actions. *Compare with* justification.

Execution

eg-zek-YOO-shun

(1) The killing of a person as criminal punishment. Executions are sometimes challenged as "cruel and unusual punishment" of the sort prohibited by the Eighth Amendment of the U.S. Constitution.

(2) The act of doing something or enforcing a plan. For example, police searching for something under a warrant are executing that warrant. Judicial enforcement of a judgment is called execution as well.

(3) An act that validates a written document. Signing a contract or will is usually required as part of its execution.

Executive branch

eg-ZEK-yoo-tiv bran'ch

The part of a government that enforces laws. U.S. presidents, state governors, and administrative agencies are executive-branch members.

Executory contract

eg-ZEK-yoo-to-ree KAHN-trakt

A contract with duties left to be performed. In bankruptcy law, a debtor may be allowed to affirm or reject its duties under such contracts going forward. Rejection allows the other party to sue for breach.

Exhibit

eg-ZIH-bit

A document or other physical object that is admitted into evidence in court. May be shown to a jury at trial, or attached to a legal memorandum during the early stages of a case.

Exigent circumstances

EG-zee-jent SUR-kuhm-stan-ses

Facts that make a situation urgent and excuse some violations of normal rules. Exigent circumstances are an exception to the Fourth Amendment's general warrant requirement. Examples are threats to life and imminent destruction of evidence.

Expectation damages

eks-peck-TAY-shun DAM-eh-jes

Money awarded to compensate a contracting party for the loss of reasonably anticipated benefits of the contract. The amount should put the contracting party where it would financially be if the contract had been performed as agreed.

Expert witness

EKS-purt WIT-nes

A witness who is qualified to present opinions at trial because of prior training, experience, technical knowledge, or skill.

Express

EKS-pres

Clearly and actually communicated. Many legal rules ask whether a statement was expressly made or whether it was merely implied.

Express authority

EKS-pres uh-THO-reh-tee

A type of actual authority that comes from a principal explicitly directing his or her agent to do some task.

Express trust

EKS-pres truh'st

A trust that is intentionally created by someone, and meets all required formalities. The person creating an express trust is called a settlor.

Express warranty

EKS-pres WOH-ren-tee

Any promise made by a buyer to a seller in connection with a sale, if it was part of the basis for the bargain. Examples may include a description of the goods, any provided samples, and promises about how they function.

Expressio unius est exclusio alterius

EKS-pre-see-oh OO-nee-oos est EKS-pre-see-oh ahl-TEHR-ee-oos

Expressly mentioned thing excludes all others. An idea that items in a list necessarily exclude items not mentioned, unless only given as examples.

Extortion

eks-TOR-shun

(1) Blackmail. Obtaining another person's property through unlawful force or threats. The threats can be oral or written.

(2) Unlawful collection of money by a public official under the color of law. This limited version of extortion used to be the only one before modern extortion laws.

F

Fact pleading
fakt PLEE-ding
A style of complaint that requires stating the ultimate facts that entitle a plaintiff to relief. This involves a greater level of specificity than notice pleading.

Fair market value
FAY'ir MAR-keht VAL-yoo
The price for which an item can be obtained on the open market. An arms-length transaction must be assumed, without a special relationship between buyer and seller.

Fair use
FAY'er yoos
Use of a copyrighted work without the author's permission, in a way that would be unlawful had it not been reasonable and limited in scope.

False imprisonment
fols im-PRIH-zon-ment
Intentional and unlawful confinement of someone to a bounded area. Can occur even if victim came voluntarily or if defendant offers some deal to free victim.

False light facts
fols lai't fakts
Statements that put someone in a false light. In other words, statements that falsely claim someone did something or believes something.

False pretenses
fols PREE-ten-ses
Obtaining title to another's property through an intentional false statement of fact, and with an intent to unlawfully keep it from the owner.

Federal question jurisdiction
FED-eh-rahl KWES-chun
The power of U.S. federal courts to hear disputes based on federal laws and treaties, or merely involving the U.S. Constitution. *See* well-pleaded complaint rule.

Federalism
FED-eh-rah-lism
A legal system with national and regional governments. Governments from different levels may carry out either different or overlapping functions.

Federal-question jurisdiction
FED-eh-rahl KWES-chun joo-ris-DIK-shun

The power of a U.S. federal court to hear cases arising under the U.S. Constitution, federal statutes, or treaties. *See* well-pleaded complaint rule.

Fee simple absolute

fee SIM'pl ab-soh-LYOOT

Unrestricted ownership of certain property. The holder of a fee simple absolute may transfer it in full, transfer a lesser ownership stake, or pass it on to beneficiaries upon death.

Fee simple determinable

fee sim'pl deh-TUR-meh-nah'bl

Ownership of certain property that may last forever, but that ends automatically if a stated event occurs, and returns to the grantor or grantor's heirs.

Fee simple subject to condition subsequent

fee sim'pl SUB-jekt too kuhn-DIH-shun sah'b-seh-KWENT

Ownership of certain property that may last forever, but that lets the grantor and grantor's heirs take it back if some stated event occurs.

Fee simple subject to executory interest

fee sim'pl SUB-jekt too eg-ZEK-yoo-to-ree INT-rest

Ownership in certain property that may last forever, but that ends automatically if a stated event occurs, and goes to someone other than grantor or grantor's heirs.

Fee tail

fee TA'yil

Ownership in certain property that may last forever, but can only pass down through lineal descendants of the grantee. Without lineal descendants, the property returns to the grantor or a third person.

Felony

FEH-lah-nee

Any crime that may be punished by death or imprisonment of more than one year. Loosely, any serious crime.

Felony murder

FEH-lah-nee MUR-der

The killing of another person during the commission of certain felonies. Relevant felonies usually include rape, arson, burglary, robbery, and kidnapping.

Fiduciary

fih-DYOO-shee-a-ree

Relating to action that must be legally done for another persons's benefit. Fiduciary duties require a sufficient level of care, good faith, diligence, and communication. A fiduciary is a person who owes such duties for the benefit of another.

Fifth Amendment

FIH'fth uh-MEND-ment

Fifth Amendment of the U.S. Constitution. It prohibits double jeopardy and compelled self-incriminating testimony in criminal cases. Also prohibits federal violations of due process.

Fighting words

FAI-ding wurds

Statements deliberately made to provoke a physically violent response from the listener. The U.S. Constitution's First Amendment does not generally protect them.

Final judgment

FAI-nuhl JUH'j-ment

An order that resolves a case on the merits and leaves nothing else that must be done except execution of the order. In general, parties can only appeal after final judgments.

Firm offer

furm AW-fur

A written offer, signed by a merchant, that cannot be withdrawn for a certain length of time. If valid, it sometimes cannot be withdrawn for three months even though offeree paid no money for this benefit.

First Amendment

furst uh-MEND-ment

First Amendment of the U.S. Constitution. It protects freedom of expression, association, and religious exercise. It also prevents establishment of a state religion.

First degree murder

furst deh-GREE MUR-der

An aggravated murder, in states that use a degree system for murder. Typically includes murders occuring during violent felonies, and murders cooly planned in advance. *See* felony murder, deliberate and premeditated murder.

Fixture

FIK's-chur

Personal property that becomes legally immovable if attached to a land or building with an intent to permanently increase the overall value.

Flat tax

flat taks

Flat rate tax. A tax that applies a single rate to things of the same category, regardless of factors such as the taxpayer's total wealth.

Forbearance

for-BEAR-uns

An intentional choice not to enforce a right. Specifically, the right may involve collection of debt or the filing of a legal claim. Debtors sometimes ask creditors for forbearance when in financial distress.

Foreclosure

for-KLOH-zhur

Legal process in which a lender holding a mortgage seizes property or forces its sale. Proceeds of the sale go toward repaying delinquent debt.

Forfeiture

FOR-feh-chur

(1) The loss of property without payment, and its acquisition by someone else. For example, criminals may be forced to forfeit property related to their crime.

(2) The loss of a right or privilege. For example, defendants may forfeit defenses by neglecting their duty to raise the defenses within a certain time.

Forgery

FOR-jeh-ree

Making a false writing with an intent to defraud someone. Includes modifying a valid writing such as a check.

Formal rulemaking

FOR-mal ROOL-may-king

A relatively slow and deliberate way to craft administrative regulations. It requires notice, formal hearings, an opportunity for interested parties to testify, and a written record.

Fornication

for-neh-CAY-shun

Open and notorious sexual relations or cohabitation between two people who are not married to each other.

Forum

FO-ruhm

(1) A place where one may deliver speeches or debate with others. *See* public forum.

(2) A court hearing a case. For example, plaintiffs sometimes wonder whether to file their complaints in a state or federal forum. *See* forum shopping.

Forum non conveniens

FO-rum nahn kahn-VEE-nee-ens

A rule allowing courts to decline some cases even if they have full jurisdiction over them. The reason for so declining is that another court appears to be a more convenient forum for parties and witnesses.

Forum shopping

FO-rum SHAH-ping

The practice of looking for the most favorable court in which to resolve a case. For example, one might look for a court with the most beneficial legal rules or the largest jury awards.

Fourteenth Amendment

FOR-teen-th uh-MEND-ment

Fourteenth Amendment of the U.S. Constitution. It prohibits states from violating principles of due process and equal protection.

Fourth Amendment

forth uh-MEND-ment

Fourth Amendment of the U.S. Constitution. It prohibits unreasonable searches and seizures. Also requires that warrants be issued with probable cause and particular descriptions.

Framing bias

FRAY-ming BAH-yus

A tendency to respond differently to the same offer depending on its phrasing. Negotiators and mediators may use the idea to speed up resolution of an issue.

Fraud (intentional misrepresentation)
fraw'd (in-TEN-shah-nul mihs-rep-rez-en-TAY-shun)
A misstatement of fact, made with reckless disregard or knowledge of falsity, with an intent to have someone rely. That someone must rely justifiably, and the misstatement causes damages.

Free exercise clause
free EKS-er-size klawz
The part of the U.S. Constitution's First Amendment that protects free exercise of religion. A burden on religion will usually be upheld only if it is a purely incidental result of a universally applicable law.

Freedom of Information Act (FOIA)
FREE-dum uhv IN-fur-may-shun akt (FOH-yah)
A U.S. federal law that sets procedures for releasing documents held by administrative agencies in response to requests from members of the public.

Freedom of speech
FREE-dum uhv spee'ch
A right to express oneself without censorship or other government restriction. Includes not only verbal speech but also symbolic actions.

Frivolous suit
FRIH-vah-lus syoot
A lawsuit without reaonable legal basis or justification. Often filed to harass or embarass the defendant.

Frolic
FRAH-lik
A significant deviation from duties. An employee who commits a tort while deviating from the scope of employment leaves the employer free of vicarious liability.

Fruit of the poisonous tree
froot uhv thuh POY-zun-us tree
A rule that if evidence is excluded at trial because it was illegally obtained, all other evidence found only because of the illegally obtained evidence should be excluded as well.

Frustration of purpose
FRUH-stray-shun uhv PUR-pus
Unforeseen change in circumstances that substantially wipes out a contracting party's essential purpose for agreeing to the contract. Such frustration terminates contractual duties owed without breach.

Full Faith and Credit Clause
fuhl feyth and KREH-dit klawz
Article IV, Section 1 of the U.S. Constitution. It requires states to legally acknowledge the acts, public records, and judicial decisions of other states.

Fundamental rights

fuhn-duh-MEN-tuhl ruy'ts

The most vital individual rights. As recognized by the U.S. Supreme Court, they include voting, personal privacy, and interstate travel. Strict scrutiny applies to laws that limit fundamental rights.

G

Gap-filler

gap FIL-ur

A rule that inserts a standard term to fill a missing piece in a contract. Courts often use gap-fillers unless the missing piece is too important to be replaced by a standard term.

Garnishment

gar-NISH-ment

Legal process through which a court may order debtors (or anyone holding debtors' property) to transfer that property to pay the debt. Thus, an employer might have to garnish an employee's wages for the employee's creditors.

General agent

JEN-eh-rahl AY-jent

An agent authorized to represent the principal in all business of a certain kind, or in all business occurring in a certain place.

General damages

JEN-eh-rahl DAM-eh-jes

Losses that are presumed from the type of injury suffered. These are losses that always occur from the injury, and do not include special circumstances peculiar to a specific injured party.

General intent

JEN-eh-rahl in-TENT

A mental state in which someone acts with awareness of all legally relevant elements. Awareness only requires knowledge of a high likelihood that something is happening or exists.

General jurisdiction

JEN-eh-rahl joo-ris-DIK-shun

(1) General subject-matter jurisdiction. A court's power to decide all types of disputes that are proper for judicial hearing. Includes civil and criminal cases.

(2) General personal jurisdiction. A court's power to render binding judgments against a defendant, even if no connections exist between the state where the court sits, the plaintiff's claims, and the defendant.

General partnership

JEN-eh-rahl PART-ner-shih'p

A type of partnership that does not offer limited liability to its partners. Thus, each partner is liable for the partnership's debts. A general partnership can arise without any written document, so long as two people intentionally run a business for profit.

General warranty deed

JEN-eh-rahl WOR-en-tee dee'd

A document that transfers property interests, and promises valid title without defects. If a third party claims ownership, grantor promises to defend title on behalf of the grantee.

Gerstein hearing

GUR-steen HEE-ring

A preliminary judicial hearing that is held after the arrest of a criminal suspect and before trial. It is supposed to confirm whether probable cause exists to detain the suspect.

Golden parachute

GOL-den para-SHOOT

An agreement that promises large benefits to an employee if the employee is fired. Usually given to high-level executive officers.

Good faith

good FAY'th

Honesty, faithful acknowledgment of promises, and observance of reasonable standards of fair dealing. Many legal rules ask whether a party showed good faith.

Goods

goo'dz

Things that are tangible and movable. Examples include cars, clothes, and most things that may be disconnected from land without material harm to the land.

Goodwill

good-WIL

The value of reputation or popularity carried by a business. Although intangible, goodwill may be reasonably estimated and converted to monetary terms.

Grand jury

grand JYOO-ree

A set of people chosen to decide whether to bring criminal charges against suspects. Grand juries have more members than trial juries, and usually sit for a fixed length of time. *See* indictment.

Gross income

GROH's IN-kum

Any addition to wealth that clearly occurs and falls under a person's control. When calculating income taxes, this is the initial number used before arriving at net income.

Gross negligence

GROH's NEG-le-jens

Negligence that falls substantially more below the proper standard of care than ordinary or "common" negligence. For example, throwing a baby in the air on a moving rollercoaster would be grossly negligent.

Guarantor

geh-ran-TOR; GAH-ran-tor

Someone who agrees to become liable for someone else's debt if the debtor misses a payment. This differs from a surety, who is immediately liable on the debt along with the debtor.

Guardian

GAR-dee-uhn

Someone with legal authority over another's life or property. Guardianship comes with a duty of care, and may exist for a specific purpose or for all purposes.

H

Habeas corpus

HAY-bee-uhs KOR-pus

Latin, "you have the body." A legal challenge used to test the legality of an arrest or detention. A *habeas corpus* writ may alert a court to one's unlawful imprisonment and result in a release.

Harmless error

HARM-les EH-ror

A mistake by a trial court that did not affect defendant's substantive rights or change the outcome of the case. Harmless error does not support reversal on appeal.

Hate crime

hay't craim

A crime in which the defendant targets a victim because the victim appears to be in a certain social group. Social groups can be based on race, religion, or sexual orientation.

Hearing

HEE-ring

An official setting in which people speak and legal decisions are made. Hearings can take place in court, before administrative agencies, or in a legislature.

Hearsay

HEER-say

A statement, made by someone other than a witness during court testimony, that is being offered to prove whatever was said in the statement. Generally not allowed at trial unless an exception applies.

Heir

A-yir

A person entitled to receive property by laws of intestacy from someone who died without a will. More loosely, anyone inheriting property from a deceased person, even if by will.

Holding

HOL-ding

(1) A court's ruling in a case; the result of applying law to facts. For nonparties to a case, holdings are the most important parts of a case because they can set a precedent for later disputes.

(2) Property that is legally owned. The sum of one's holdings is equal to the dollar amount of all real property and personal property owned.

Holographic will

hah-luh-GRA-fik will

A will that is handwritten by the testator and can lack signing witnesses. Legally recognized in about half of U.S. states.

Homestead law

HOE'm-sted law

A law that protects one's residential property from seizure by creditors. Exceptions exist, such as when a husband and wife jointly grant a security interest in their house.

Homicide

HAH-mih-sai'd

The killing of a person by another person. Only criminal homicide is punished. Justifiable and excusable homicides are not punished.

Hung jury

HUH'ng JYOO-ree

A jury whose members cannot agree on a verdict with the number of votes required for that particular crminal charge.

Hybrid rulemaking

HAI-bryd ROOL-may-king

A way to craft administrative regulations that mixes elements of formal and informal rulemaking. Thus, a hearing may be held, but without any strict rules for submitting evidence.

I

Immunity

ee-MYOO-nee-tee

Any shield or exemption from something. In specific contexts:

(1) Any exemption from liability possessed by virtue of one's position or power. Many government officials, charities, and family members of the plaintiff cannot be held liable for torts.

(2) Any exemption from liability that is specifically granted. In criminal cases, witnesses often get immunity from prosecution so they can be compelled to testify about some criminal event.

Impartiality

im-par-she-A-lee-tee

Lack of bias or interest in how something gets resolved. Judges and other decision-makers should be fully impartial unless otherwise agreed by all parties involved.

Impeachment

im-PEECH-ment

(1) Formal accusation of misconduct by a legislature against a public official. After deciding to impeach, the legislature holds hearings, and votes on whether to remove the public official from office.

(2) The casting of doubt on the credibility of a trial witness. Proving a lie or highlighting inconsistent testimony are popular ways to discredit a witness.

Impleader

im-PLEE-der

A procedure to bring new parties into a lawsuit. For example, a defendant who thinks someone else caused plaintiff's injury should implead the other party.

Implied

im-PLAH'id

Not actually or clearly communicated. Instead, it is something that can be inferred from other facts. Many legal rules give effect to implied statements or actions.

Implied authority

im-PLAH'id uh-THO-reh-tee

A type of actual authority that is reasonably inferred from a principal's actions. For instance, express authority to walk a dog implies authority to put it on a leash.

Implied trust

im-PLAH'id truh'st

A trust that arises even though an intent to create one was not expressed. There are two types of implied trusts. *See* resulting trust, constructive trust.

Implied warranty of fitness for a particular purpose

im-PLAH'id WOH-ren-tee uhv fit-nes for a par-TIK-yoo-lar PUR-pus

A promise that goods are fit for a special purpose. This promise is presumed when a seller knows about the special purpose, should know that buyer is relying on seller's skill in selecting the proper goods, and buyer really does rely.

Implied warranty of habitability
im-PLAH'id WOH-ren-tee uhv ha-bih-tah-BIL-ee-tee
In some jurisdictions, a rule read into a lease contract even if not actually there. It obligates landlords to make residential property reasonably suitable for human life.

Implied warranty of merchantability
im-PLAH'id WOH-ren-tee uhv mur-chent-ah-BIL-ih-tee
A set of promises presumed when a merchant sells goods. The most important promise is that the goods are fit for their ordinary purposes.

Implied-in-fact contract
im-PLAH'id in fakt KAHN-trakt
An agreement formed by conduct rather than spoken or written words. For example, sitting down in a barbershop is sufficient to form a contract once the barber starts cutting hair.

Impossibility
im-pah-sih-BIH-lih-tee
State of events which prevent something from being done. Valid impossibilities excuse performance of a contract. Examples include death of a party, or the destruction of irreplaceable tools.

Impracticability
im-PRAK-tih-kah-bih-lih-tee
A difficulty that may excuse performance of a contract if legally recognized to be valid. Such difficulties usually need to be unforeseen and very serious.

In absentia
in ab-SEN-shah; in ab-SEN-chee-yah
In one's absence. For example, a trial *in absentia* is one held without the defendant being present. In the U.S., no prosecution may begin without a defendant being present.

In camera
in KA-meh-rah
In a judge's office, or in the courtroom without a jury or spectators present. Can also refer to judicial action that occurs anytime court is not in session.

In limine
in LIM-eh-nee
"At the outset." For example, a motion *in limine* might be presented in the judge's office early in a trial to decide whether the jury can see a piece of evidence.

In loco parentis
in low-ko pah-REN-tis
"In place of a parent." Refers to responsibility or action taken while temporarily acting as one's guardian.

Teachers may act *in loco parentis* during school hours.

In pari delicto
in PAH-ree deh-LIK-tow
"In equal fault." A court may refuse to grant any relief to the parties in a case if they were *in pari delicto*.

In rem jurisdiction
in rehm joo-ris-DIK-shun
A court's power over a certain piece of property. A court with such power may seize that property and hold a trial to decide who owns it.

Incest
IN-sest
Sexual relations between close relatives. Typically includes relations between parents and children related by adoption.

Inchoate offense
in-KOH-et ah-FENS
A type of crime that involved something in the early stages; that would have produced a further result if completed. *See* solicitation, attempt, conspiracy.

Incidental damages
in-sih-DEN-tal DAM-eh-jes
Losses reasonably related to actual damages. For a buyer rejecting defective goods, incidental damages include money spent to inspect and ship the goods back.

Income beneficiary
in-KUHM beh-neh-FIH-shuh-ree
Someone who may or must receive income raised from trust assets. Unlike a remainder beneficiary, seeks larger income disbursements, and worries less about aggressive investments.

Income tax
IN-kum taks
A charge by the government that is based on the amount of cash or other wealth received in a year.

Incompetency to stand trial
in-KAHM-peh-ten-see too stand TRAI-yul
A lack of ability to understand criminal charges and proceedings, along with insufficient ability to consult with one's lawyer.

Incorporation
in-kor-puh-RAY-shun
(1) Legal process for creating a corporation. Includes paperwork, fees, filing, and approval by the relevant public official.
(2) Legal process for recognizing a regional or city government under the laws of a country or state.
(3) The decision to apply a federal constitutional Amendment to the government of each U.S. state. This works by finding that Fourteenth-Amendment due process (which expressly applies to state governments) requires states

to protect civil rights listed in that Amendment.

Inculpatory evidence
in-KUL-pah-to-ree EH-vih-dens

Evidence that tends to prove someone's involvement in committing a crime. One example is proof of a loud argument between a defendant and a murder victim.

Indemnification
in-dem-nih-fih-KAY-shun

Compensation for loss. Often refers to a payment, made in accordance with a prior contract, that reimburses a losing defendant for the damages awarded in a case.

Independent contractor
in-DUH-pen-dunt KAHN-trakt

Someone hired to perform a project but left free to choose the details and manner of performance.

Indictment
in-DAI't-ment

A formal criminal charge issued by a grand jury and presented to a court. The U.S. Constitution's Fifth Amendment requires indictments for some types of prosecutions.

Indigent
IN-dih-jent

Lacking the means for basic necessities of life. Indigent criminal defendants are usually entitled to an attorney at public cost.

Infancy
IN-fun-see

(1) Period of life when one is under legal age for entering binding contracts, for automatic prosecution as an adult, or for something else. Also called minority.

(2) Early stages of anything, such as the first few years of life.

Informal rulemaking
in-FOR-mal ROOL-may-king

A relatively fast and simple way to craft administrative regulations. It requires only notice and an opportunity for interested parties to send comments before the regulation takes effect.

Informant
in-FOR-mant

Someone who provides information against another's interests. Most often refers to someone who supplies confidential information to the police.

Informed consent
in-FORM'd KAHN-sent

Permission or approval that is given only after knowing sufficient information about the material risks and reasonable alternatives to proposed action.

Infringement

in-FRIN'j-ment

Violation of one's right. Most often refers to violations of constitutional rights, as well as violations of intellectual property rights.

Inherent authority

in-HERR-ent uh-THO-reh-tee

Authority that is not actually given or apparent, yet still legally binding on the principal. Thus, an agent exceeding his powers can make the principal liable for damages out of considerations of fairness to third-parties.

Inheritance

in-HEH-reh-tens

Property passed down from an ancestor, either by a will, or by laws of intestacy from ancestors who died without a will. Loosely, anything passed down to another person or caretaker.

Injunction

in-JUNK-shun

An order by a court that requires or forbids certain action. To win an injunction, a party must show a threat of irreperable harm that cannot be compensated by money damages.

Insanity defense

in-SA-nee-tee deh-FENS

A defense that relieves criminal defendants of liability if a mental disease or defect caused their actions. Such defendants are usually confined to psychiatric institution. *See* M'Naghten rule, Irresistible impulse test, *Durham* test, MPC insanity test.

Insider trading

in-SAH'y-der TRAY-ding

Buying or selling of a corporation's stock by someone who can access the corporation's internal and undisclosed information. Insider trading is heavily regulated to prevent fraud.

Installment method

in-STOL-ment MEH-thud

Accounting method that splits income from property sales into separate tax periods. It is sometimes used when the buyer pays gradually over time.

Insurance

in-SHU-rens

An agreement by which someone promises to pay for another party's loss, damage, or liability. The other party typically pays regularly for this promise.

Intangible

in-TAN-jih-bul

Incapable of being physically touched. Often refers to things of value (such as patents and goodwill) that cannot be touched. These are called intangible property, or simply "intangibles."

Integration

in-teh-GRAY-shun

Combining multiple things into one. For instance, courts should find that all papers intended as part of a will are integrated into it. Likewise, an integrated contract is one that contains all terms of a bargain.

Intent
in-TENT

The mental decision to perform an act. Intent differs from motive, which is a reason that may persuade someone to form an intent.

Intentional infliction of emotional distress (IIED)
in-TEN-shuh-nahl in-FLIK-shun uhv ee-MOW-shuh-nahl dis-TREH's (ai ai ee dee)

Behavior that is extreme and outrageous. Defendant must be reckless about how it affects another person, or actually intend and cause severe emotional distress to a person.

Intentional tort
in-TEN-shah-nul tor't

Category of torts that involve unlawful acts done voluntarily and deliberately. Examples include battery, assault, false imprisonment, and trespass.

Inter vivos
IN-tur VAI-vos

Between living people. Refers to property transfers that take place during the grantor's lifetime. This contrasts with transfers made upon death, or in contemplation of imminent death.

Interest
INT-rest

(1) Involvement in a matter, or a desire to have something happen.

(2) An ownership stake or share in some property.

(3) Compensation for the use of money, such as that paid to a lending bank. Interest rates are calculated as a fixed or variable percentage of the borrowed amount.

Interested witness
INT-res-ted WIT-nes

A signing witness to someone's will who receives a benefit under the will. Historically, such witness was disqualified and the wiill might be invalid. Modern laws keep the will valid, but sometimes decrease benefits to interested witnesses.

Interlocutory order
in-tur-LAHK-yoo-to-ree OR-der

A court's intermediate order in a case. This includes all orders except final judgments. Parties can rarely appeal directly from interlocutory orders.

Intermediate scrutiny
inter-MEE-dee-yet SKROO-t'nee

A test asking whether government action is substantially related to an important government purpose. A law properly subjected to this test and found lacking is invalid.

Interpleader
in-tur-PLEE-der
A lawsuit filed by someone holding property with the goal of conclusively determining who owns that property. This prevents future lawsuits from interested parties.

Interrogatory
in-teh-RAH-gah-to-ree
A question sent to an opposing party in a case, in preparation for a possible trial. Multiple interrogatories are usually sent together in one document.

Intervening force
in-tur-VEE-ning fors
An independent cause that arises after an earier cause and combines with it to produce a result. In tort cases, intervening forces generally do not cut off liability if the result was foreseeable.

Intervention
in-ter-VEN-shun
Voluntary and deliberate entry of a new party into a lawsuit. The goal is to prevent harm to the intervenor even though he or she was not originally included in the case.

Intestate
in-TEH-stay't
A person who dies without leaving a valid will. A state's laws of intestacy govern the distribution of such person's property. Spouses and children are the first heirs in line to receive property.

Intoxication
in-tahk-sih-KAY-shun
Decreased mental and physical abilities due to alcohol or other drugs. Intoxication may be a defense to some unlawful actions. *See* voluntary intoxication, involuntary intoxication.

Intrusion
in-TROO-zhun
Entrance or interference. May be physical, as in a trespass. May also be more intangible, as when someone invades another's privacy.

Invitee
in-vai-TEE
Someone expressly invited to enter another person's land. The owner invites the person for the owner's benefit, or else specifically makes the property open to the public at large.

Involuntary intoxication
in-VAH-luhn-ta-ree in-tahk-sih-KAY-shun
Influence from alcohol or other drugs consumed or injected against one's will. Can always be a defense to unlawful actions by one so influenced.

Involuntary manslaughter
in-VAH-luhn-ta-ree MAN-slaw-tur
Murder by criminal negligence or an unlawful intentional act. Criminal negligence requires a bigger failure to meet a standard of care than civil negligence. Unlawful acts include some felonies and misdemeanors.

Irresistible impulse test
eer-eh-ZIS-tih'bl eem-puls test
Insanity defense requiring that defendant had a mental illness that prevented an ability to control actions or conform to legal requirements.

Issue
ISH-yoo
(1) A disputed question. Every lawsuit involves at least one issue being disputed between two or more parties.
(2) In wills and estates, the lineal descendants of people. The term "lawful issue" includes not only children but also descendants of younger generations.

J

Joinder

JOY'n-dur

Addition of new claims or parties that were not in the original complaint. It allows plaintiffs to modify their cases as they change strategies or discover new facts.

Joint and several liability

JOY'nt and SEH-veh-rahl lah-yah-BIH-leh-tee

Responsibility of multiple parties whose actions combined to cause a single, indivisible injury. Plaintiff can demand full damages from any one of the parties. *See* contribution.

Joint causes

JOY'nt KAW-zez

Two or more facts that bring about a result. Either one would be sufficient to produce the result on its own. Each is an actual cause as long as it was a substantial factor behind the result.

Joint tenancy

JOY'nt TEH-nan-see

Ownership in certain property that is held by two or more people. Such owners must obtain their united interest to jointly possess property at the same time, and in the same document.

Joint venture

JOY'nt VEN-chur

An association of two or more people who intend to make joint profit by engaging in a single business venture. Each member should have some ability to control the project and be prepared to share any losses.

Judge

JUH'j

A public official that decides legal disputes. Must be objective and neutral. Judges serving under Article III of the U.S. Constitution are appointed for life.

Judgment

JUH'j-ment

A court's conclusion on some disputed issue. Judgments may include monetary awards and equitable remedies such as injunctions or specific performance.

Judgment as a matter of law (JMOL)

JUH'j-ment az a MA-tur uhv law (jay em oh el)

A court's ruling for one party because no legally sufficient reason exists for another conclusion. Can be issued before the jury deliberates (like a directed verdict), or can override the jury's verdict.

Judgment notwithstanding the verdict (JNOV)

JUH'j-ment naht-with-STAN-ding thuh VER-dee'kt (jay en oh vee)

A court's ruling for one party even though the jury ruled against that party. It overrides the jury's verdict because the jury failed to analyze the evidence in a legally permissible way.

Judgment on the pleadings
JUH'j-ment ahn thuh PLEE-dings
A court's ruling that is based only on information contained in the parties' pleadings. Motions for such judgments can come as soon the pleading stage of a case is closed.

Judicial branch
joo-DIH-shul bran'ch
The part of a government that interprets laws and applies them to resolve disputes. The U.S. Supreme Court and other courts are judicial institutions.

Judicial notice
joo-DIH-shul NO-tis
A judge's recognition that something is true without the need to formally present evidence. For example, a judge must recognize federal statutes without requiring testimony from legislators who passed them.

Jurisdiction
joo-ris-DIK-shun
(1) Power to exercise political or judicial authority. Jurisdiction comes in different forms. *See, e.g.*, subject-matter jursdiction, personal jursdiction.
(2) Geographic area in which government authority may be exercised. For example, the U.S. as a whole and each of the U.S. states is a separate jurisdiction with legal differences from the others.

Jury
JYOO-ree
A set of people chosen to decide questions of fact in a court case. The judge still decides questions of law. Jury verdicts can be overturned if not based on legally sufficient evidence.

Jury instructions
JYOO-ree in-STRAHK-shuns
Rules or directions given to juries by judges, especially right before deliberations. They concern ideas such as burden of proof and witness credibility.

Jury trial
JYOO-ree TRAI-yul
A trial in which jury members resolve questions of fact, not a judge. There is no U.S. federal right to jury trial for minor crimes; only for offenses that could result in at least six months' imprisonment.

Jus sanguinis
yoos SAHN-gwih-nis
"By right of the blood." A rule that passes citizenship down from parents to children, regardless of where a child is born. *Compare with jus soli.*

Jus soli

yoos SOW-lee

"By right of the soil." A rule making anyone born in a country a citizen of that country. The Fourteenth Amendment of the U.S. Constitution includes this rule. *Compare with jus sanguinis.*

Justiciability

juh-stee-shuh-BIH-luh-tee

The question of whether some grievance is appropriate for judicial hearing. Various justiciability rules exist. *See* standing, ripeness, mootness.

Justification

jahs-tih-fih-KAY-shun

A defense that leaves people blameless because their actions were proper and correct under the circumstances. *Compare with* excuse.

K

Kidnapping
KIHD-na-ping
Unlawful movement of a victim, or the unlawful hiding of a victim in a secret place. At common law, also required moving the victim to a different country.

Knock and announce rule
nahk and ah-NAH-oons rool
Requirement for police executing a search warrant to knock and announce themselves. Still, exceptions such as risk of destroyed evidence apply, and evidence seized in violation is not excluded.

Knockout rule
NAHK-ah'oot rool
The idea that contradictory terms in an offer and acceptance do not end up in the contract. Each party is assumed to object to the other's terms, and a gap exists which may be filled. *See* gap-filler.

Knowingly
NO-in-glee
Doing something with the awareness of doing it. Acting with knowledge that the action will likely or certainly produce some result.

L

Labor union

YOON-yun

Organization of workers from a certain company or entire profession. The organization has powers such as collective bargaining, which is backed up by the threat of strikes. Also called trade union, or simply "union."

Laches

LA-tches

A defense that claims plaintiff should lose the case because of unreasonable delay in bringing the claim. For this defense to succeed, the delay must have prejudiced the defendant.

Larceny

LAR-seh-nee

Taking and carrying away another person's tangible personal property unlawfully, intending to keep it from the owner at least for an unreasonable time.

Larceny by trick

LAR-seh-nee bai trik

Obtaining possession of another's property through an intentional false statement of fact, and with an intent to unlawfully keep it from the owner.

Lawsuit

LAW-syoot

Any proceeding between competing parties in court. Also called suit, action, or case.

Lawyer

LOH-yer

Someone legally permitted to work as an adviser and representative on legal matters for other people. Lawyers must be licensed or given limited scope to work in a state where they provide services.

Lay witness

lay WIT-nes

Any witness who is not testifying as an expert witness. Only allowed to re-tell directly observed facts, and state very general opinions that do not require technical knowledge.

Leading question

LEE-ding KWES-chun

A question at trial that makes a factual claim, and usually aims for a quick "yes" or "no" from the witness. Generally prohibited during direct examination.

Lease

lees

A right to use and occupy property. The right is usually granted in exchange for payment of rent. May be granted by an unrestricted owner or anyone else in rightful possession.

Legacy
LEH-gah-see
Property transferred through a will upon one's death. Usually refers to personal property (most commonly money). *See* bequest, devise.

Legal secretary
LEE-gahl SEH-kreh-ta-ree
Someone skilled in formatting documents, filing court papers, scheduling meetings, and many other activities required for legal practice.

Legislative branch
LEH-jus-lay-tiv bran'ch
The part of a government that passes laws. The U.S. Congress and state legislatures are examples.

Lesser included offense
LEH-sur IN-klyoo-ded ah-FENS
A crime that consists totally of elements that are also required for another crime. The other crime should require at least one other element not needed by this one.

Levy
LEH-vee
(1) Legally proper seizure and sale of property. In the typical case, a sheriff's levy on defendant's property will satisfy a money judgment against the defendant.
(2) Imposition of a tax, fine, or surcharge on something. Many countries levy high taxes on imported goods.

Lex loci
leks LOW-kai
"The law of the place." The local law in a place where something occurred. Such law may differ from the law where the trial occurs.

Lex loci contractus
leks LOW-kai KAHN-trak-tus
The law of the place where a contract was executed, or where the duties owed under contract were supposed to be performed.

Lex loci delicti
leks LOW-kai deh-LIK-tee
The law of the place where a crime or tort occurred. This may differ from the law where the trial occurs, or the law where someone conspired to commit the unlawful act.

Liability
lah-yah-BIH-leh-tee
Legal obligation that is enforceable in court. Criminal liability may lead to prosecution and punishment. Civil liability may lead to lawsuits and damages.

Liability insurance

lah-yah-BIH-leh-tee in-SHU-rens

Insurance that covers all amounts an insured party must legally pay. Such amounts may include property damage and personal injuries.

License

LAI-sens

Permission to do something that is unlawful without such permission. Includes such things as a driver license, and a license to manufacture patent-protected goods.

Licensee

lai-sen-SEE

In general, anyone who is granted a license to do something. In property law, someone allowed to enter another person's land due to personal interests.

Lien

leen

A creditor's security interest in property, held until the owner fulfills an obligation. Many liens are created and publicly recorded by providers of professional services.

Life estate

laif eh-STAY't

Ownership in certain property that only lasts until one's death. The relevant death may be that of the grantee, or of a different person altogether.

Limited admissibility

LIH-mit-ed ad-mih-sih-BIH-lee-tee

A way to admit evidence at trial for one purpose, but not for another. For example, a prior conviction may throw doubt on someone's credibility, but cannot be used as evidence that he is guilty of current charges.

Limited jurisdiction

LEEM-eh-ted joo-ris-DIK-shun

Limited subject-matter jurisdiction. A court's power to hear only certain types of cases. For example, a state's Tax Court might only have power to resolve tax disputes and no other cases.

Limited liability company (LLC)

LYM-eh-ted lah-yah-BIH-leh-tee KUM-pah-nee

A business organization that blends the limited liability of corporations with the governing rules and taxation benefits of partnerships. May be formed where authorized by state law.

Limited liability partnership

LIH-mit-ed lah-yah-BIH-leh-tee

A type of partnership that limits a partner's liability for professional malpractice not involving that partner. A written statement of qualification must be filed with the state to create it.

Limited partnership

LIM-eh-ted PART-ner-shih'p

A type of partnership that offers limited liability to at least some of the partners involved. Limited partners are only liable for partnership debts to the extent of their investment. A written certificate of partnership must be filed with the state to create a limited partnership.

Lineup

LAIN-ahp

An identification tool used by the police. A suspect and physically similar people are lined up together. A victim or witness is then asked if he can identify the person who committed the crime.

Liquidated damages

LIH-kwih-day-ted DAM-eh-jes

An amount agreed in advance by contracting parties as a reasonable estimate of damages for breach. Liquidated damages are appropriate if calculating actual damages after the fact would be too difficult or impossible.

Liquidation

lih-kwi-DAY-shun

(1) The selling of non-cash assets to obtain cash. Often sold at auction to satisfy debts.

(2) Calculation of an exact amount of debt or damages. May be found by agreement or litigation. *See, e.g.,* liquidated damages.

Living will

LIH-ving wil

A document, made with the formalities of a will, which specifies what life-prolonging measures may and may not be used if one becomes incapacitated without a reasonable expectation of recovery.

Long-arm statute

LAW'ng ahr'm STA'tch-yoot

A type of state law that authorizes courts to exercise personal jurisdiction over anyone, as long as the Due Process Clause of the Fourteenth Amendment is not violated.

Loss of consortium

loh's uhv kahn-SOR-shum

Benefits enjoyed between two close people, especially spouses. May include help, companionship, financial support, and sexual relations.

Lost volume seller

law'st VAH'l-yoom seh-LER

Someone who can theoretically sell as much of an identical item as it wishes. If a buyer breaches a contract to buy such item, he is liable for full lost profits. Damages will not decrease simply because seller sold the item to someone else.

M

***M'Naghten* rule**

mik-NAWT'n rool

Insanity defense requiring that defendant had a mental disease that caused a problem in reasoning so that defendant did not understand wrongfulness of actions or their nature and quality. Also spelled McNaghten and M'Naughten.

Magistrate

MEH-jis-tray't

An official with powers that are strictly limited by whatever document creates his or her position. For example, neutral judicial magistrates exist whose sole power is to decide whether to issue warrants.

Mailbox rule

MA'yel-box rul

A principle through which a contract arises once the acceptance of an offer is properly dropped in the mail. This rule does not apply if the offer makes acceptance valid only upon actual arrival.

Malfeasance

mal-FEE-zens

Wrongdoing. May refer to unlawful action of a public official or private individual. Differs slightly from misfeasance, which can refer to a lawful act done in an unlawful way. *Compare with* nonfeasance.

Malice

MA-lis

(1) Intent to commit a wrongful act. Requires absence of any excuse or justification.
(2) In the context of defamation, defendant's knowledge that a communicated statement is false, or reckless disregard of whether it is true or not.

Malice aforethought

MEH-lis a-FOR-thawt

An element required for a homicide to be murder. Any of these count as malice aforethought: intent to kill, intent to cause great bodily harm, intent to commit a felony, or reckless indifference to an unjustifiably high risk of injury.

Malicious prosecution

MAH-lih-shus prah-see-KYOO-shun

Putting in motion a criminal case against someone, without proper purpose and without probable cause of guilt. Acquitted criminal defendants can sue for such action.

Malpractice

mal-PRAK-tis

Failure by a professional to meet an appropriate standard of care or competence. Medical and legal malpractice are common examples.

Malum in se
MAH-loom in sey

Wrong in itself. Refers to crimes that are obviously or inherently evil. Examples include murder and rape. *Compare with malum prohibitum.*

Malum prohibitum
MAH-loom prah-HIH-bih-tum

Wrong only because prohibited by law. Refers to crimes that are not inherently evil, but are defined as crimes. One example is drug use by informed adults. *Compare with malum in se.*

Manager
MAN-uh-jer

In a limited liability company (LLC), someone appointed by the owners to run business operations along with other managers.

Mandatory authority
MAN-duh-to-ree uh-THO-reh-tee

Legal precedents that are binding on the court deciding a case. Includes decisions of all higher courts that have appellate authority over the court deciding a case.

Mandatory jurisdiction
MAN-duh-tori joo-ris-DIK-shun

A court's obligation to hear a case if it has jurisdiction over the subject-matter and parties. Courts have no power to decline a case if such obligation applies.

Manufacturing defect
man-yoo-FAK-choo-ring DEE-fekt

A problem with how one specific item is made, so that it is different and more dangerous than others of the same product line. *Compare with* design defect.

Material
mah-TEE-ree-ul

Sufficiently significant for a given purpose. For example, the way someone is dressed is usually immaterial when asking if they committed a crime.

Material breach
muh-TEE-rih-yahl BREE'ch

A breach of contract that so impairs the value of the entire agreement that the injured party is excused from performing and may sue for damages.

Mathews v. Eldridge test
MA-thyus vee EL-dridge test

A test for determining how and when administrative agencies should allow persons to respond before affecting their interests. Factors include government interest, the person's interest, the risk of errorenous action, and the value of additional safeguards.

Means of representation

meenz uhv rep-rez-en-TAY-shun

Tools and procedural steps used by a lawyer when trying to achieve the client's objectives of representation. Lawyers are solely responsible for picking which means are used.

Measuring life

MEH-zhu-ring laif

Under the rule against perpetuities, a person who was alive at the time of a conveyance, and after whose death someone's contingent interest must be sure to vest within 21 years or else be cancelled.

Mediation

mee-dee-A-shun

Attempt to resolve disputes out of court with the help of a neutral third party. The process itself is not binding, although it can lead to binding voluntary agreements.

Member

MEM-buhr

In a limited liability company (LLC), owners who are automatically authorized to run business operations by virtue of their ownership.

Memorandum

meh-mah-RAN-duhm

(1) A document that formally presents one's legal arguments in court. A brief is one type of memorandum.

(2) A document that contains key terms of a contract or transaction in written form.

(3) A piece of communication between people working in the same office. Often shortened to "inter-office memo."

Mens rea

mens RAY'ah

The mental element of a crime. It refers to a certain intent or mental state that constitutes a crime when coupled with a certain action. *See actus reus.*

Merchant

MUR-chent

Someone who regularly buys or sells certain types of things. In addition, people who do not regularly buy or sell anything, but who by virtue of their job seem to have special knowledge or skills about certain types of things or services.

Merger

MUR-jer

In general, the combination of multiple things into one. In specific contexts:

1) Absorption of one business into another (both are usually corporations). The absorbed business no longer exists; its assets and liabilities pass to the other business.

2) Absorption of a lesser criminal charge into a more serious one. For instance, one cannot be convicted of an attempt to rob a store and the robbery of the same store based on the same events.

3) Absorption of a lesser property estate into a greater one when a single owner acquires both. Thus, someone with a life estate in property owns it without restriction after buying a fee simple absolute in the same property.

Minimum contacts

MIN-eh-mum KAHN-tak'ts

One way for a court to have personal jurisdiction over a party. Through minimum contacts with a state (e.g., past business deals), a party may be unwillingly brought into a court case.

Mini-trial

MIH-nee TRAI-yul

A form of alternative dispute resolution. A private, voluntary, and relatively short version of what would happen in court between the parties. The goal is to reach a settelement.

Minor breach

MY-nor BREE'ch

A breach of contract that is relatively small. It does not impair the value of the entire agreement enough to excuse the injured party from performing. The injured party can demand that the breach be cured and is allowed to sue for damages.

***Miranda* warning**

mee-RAN-dah WAR-ning

Set of items that must be told to a person undergoing custodial interrogation by the police, if the Fifth Amendment applies. The items mention and clarify the right to stay silent and the right to an attorney.

Mirror image rule

MIH-ror EH-maj rool

A requirement that the valid acceptance of an offer cannot change, delete, or add anything to the terms of the offer. In most cases, the mirror image rule no longer applies in full.

Misdemeanor

MIS-dee-mee-nor

Any crime that can be punished at most by a fine, penalty, restitution, or imprisonment of less than a year. Loosely, any relatively minor crime.

Misprision

mis-PREE-zhun

Failure to carry out a duty. For example, misprision of a felony would be a failure to report someone else's serious crime. Misprision of a felony is no longer a crime under most U.S. laws.

Mistake of fact

mihs-TAYK uhv law

A mistake about some legally significant fact. May be a valid defense to some criminal charges and tort claims.

Mistake of law

mihs-TAYK uhv law

Lack of knowledge about the legal effect of behavior. In general, ignorace of the law is no defense. Still, a mistake of law may be a valid defense, as when a senior public official incorrectly interprets the law for someone.

Mitigating circumstance

mih-tih-GAY-ting SUR-kuhm-stens

A fact or reason that makes action less blameworthy, decreases degree of liability, or leads to smaller punishment.

Mock trial

mahk TRAI-yul

Fictitious presentation that simulates a trial. Often held by attorneys as practice for a specific upcoming trial in court. May also be created with fully fictitious facts to practice general trial techniques.

Model Penal Code (MPC)

MAH-del PEE-nahl KOH-d (em pee see)

A proposed system of criminal laws produced by the American Law Institute in 1962. Adopted, at least in part, by many U.S. states.

Mootness

MOOT-nes

The resolution of a dispute such that a judicial decision will be meaningless. A case is not moot if the issues tend to evade judicial review but tend to repeat.

Moral turpitude

MO-rahl TUR-pih-tyood

An act or characteristic that shows a tendency to be dishonest, immoral, or depraved. Crimes of moral turpitude include perjury and murder.

Mortgage

MOR-gej

A security interest in property given as collateral for a loan or other obligation. In many cases, the loan involved was obtained to purchase the property.

Motion

MOW-shun

Official request or application for a certain decision in court. For example, a party wishing to win a case without trial may file a motion for summary judgment. Someone filing a motion can also be said to "move" for whatever is being requested.

Motion to dismiss

MOW-shun too dis-MIS

Official request to terminate a court's handling of a case. Such motion usually argues that the court lacks jurisdiction or that the plaintiff cannot win even if all allegations are true.

Motion to remand

MOW-shun too ree-MAND

Official request to send something back for more review. For example, after a defendant removes a case from state to federal court, the plaintiff can argue to send it back in a motion to remand.

Motion to strike

MOW-shun too STRAI'k

Request to a court, asking to officially delete part of an opponent's pleading. Alleged facts, claims, and defenses may all be struck for insufficiency or scandalous content.

Motive
MO-tiv
A reason that may persuade someone to do something. A beneficiary under a life insurance policy may have a motive to secretly kill the person insured.

MPC insanity test
em pee see in-SA-nee-tee test
Insanity defense requiring that defendant had a mental problem preventing substantial capacity to either understand criminality of actions, or conform to legal requirements. Also known as the American Law Institute (ALI) test.

Murder
MUR-der
Unlawful killing of a person by another, with malice aforethought. Any of these mental states prove malice aforethought: intent to kill, intent to cause great bodily harm, intent to commit a felony, or reckless indifference to an unjustifiably high risk of injury.

Mutual assent
MYOO-tchoo-ahl uh-sent
Agreement by multiple parties to the essential terms of a proposal. In the ususal case, mutual assent occurs when someone extends an offer and someone else accepts it.

Mutual mistake
MYOO-tchoo-ahl mihs-TAYK
Mistake of fact by both parties to a contract. A party hurt by such mistake can usually void the contract if it did not assume the risk of mistake, and the mistake materially affected the bargain and concerned a basic assumption of the agreement.

Mutual misunderstanding
MYOO-tchoo-ahl mihs-uhn-der-STAN-ding
An expression that seems clear to all contracting parties, but later turns out to be ambiguous. A classic case involved two ships named Peerless, with each party contemplating a different ship. Also called latent ambiguity mistake.

Mutuality
myoo-tchoo-A-lity
State of events in which something exists on two or more sides. A valid contract requires mutual consideration on both sides. In other words, both parties must have obligations or else one side's promise is illusory.

N

Natural condition

NA-chu-rahl

Something that exists naturally, without human intervention. Landowners have different responsibilities to warn of dangerious natural conditions than artificial conditions.

Necessary and Proper Clause

NEH-suh-sah-ree and PRAH-pur klawz

Article I, Section 8, Clause 18 of the U.S. Constitution. It lets Congress pass any law reasonably related to one of its expressly granted constitutional powers.

Necessity

neh-SEH-sih-tee

(1) In torts, a privilege that allows one to harm property without liability if this was the only way to protect life or health. Still, money damages may need to be paid.

(2) In criminal law, a defense for someone who acted in an emergency and prevented a lesser harm than he caused. For the defense to work, defendant could not have created the emergency in the first place.

Negligence

NEG-le-jens

Breach of legal duty to conform to a standard of care. To make defendant liable, the breach must be an actual and proximate cause of plaintiff's injuries.

Negligent infliction of emotional distress (NIED)

NEG-le-jent in-FLIK-shun uhv ee-MOW-shuh-nahl dis-TREH's (en ai ee dee)

Breach of a duty of care toward someone, resulting in emotional distress from the possibility of physical harm, or severe emotional distress on its own.

Negligent misrepresentation

NEG-le-jent mihs-rep-rez-en-TAY-shun

A misstatement of fact, in a commercial setting, which is a breach of duty toward an injured party who justifiably relied on the statement, and which causes damages.

Next of kin

neh'kst uhv kih'n

The person or people most closely related to someone who has died. May be related by blood lineage or other reason.

Nexus

NEK-sus

A connection between events or concepts. Often, one thing causes another. For example, a private party infringing on rights must have a close nexus with the federal government for the Bill of Rights to apply.

Nolo contendere (no contest)
NOH-low kuhn-TEN-deh-ree (no KAHN-test)
A criminal plea through which defendants decline to dispute charges while stopping short of admitting guilt. Although it can be strategically advantageous, it is not always available in every case.

Nominal damages
NAH-mi-nahl DAM-eh-jes
A tiny amount of money awarded if an injury legally occurred but caused no harm for which compensation is owed. It serves as technical acknowledgment that defendant's actions were wrong.

Nonconforming goods
nahn-kahn-FOR-ming goo'dz
Items that do not meet the terms or standards named in a contract. Under the Uniform Commercial Code, even the slightest nonconformance gives buyer an option to reject.

Nonfeasance
nahn-FEE-zens
Unlawful failure to act. Refers to action that was not done despite being legally required. *Compare with* malfeasance.

Non-obviousness
nahn AHB-vee-yus-nes
In patent law, a requirement that a new invention must go sufficiently beyond existing knowledge so that it would not be easily apparent to an ordinary person in the same industry.

Notarization
no-tah-reh-ZAY-shun
A way to record the authenticity of a document by having a publicly recognized official vouch for it. The official is called a notary public.

Notice and comment
NO-tis and KAH-ment
A process by which government bodies inform the public of proposed action, and then set aside time to receive comments from interested parties.

Notice pleading
NO-tis PLEE-ding
A style of complaint that is simple and direct. The idea is to put the defendant on notice of general claims. U.S. federal courts require notice pleading. *Compare with* fact pleading.

Notice statute
NO-tis STA'tch-yoot
A recording act that gives title to a later good-faith buyer rather than an earlier buyer who failed to record the purchase.

Novation

no-VAY-shun

The replacement of an old contractual arrangement with a new one. The new arrangement may involve different duties, different parties, or both.

Novelty

NAH-vel-tee

The quality of being new. To qualify for a patent, an invention should be novel. This means it cannot have been publicly disclosed or already patented.

Nuisance

NYOO-sens

An activity or condition that infringes on another's right to use and enjoy property. Examples include loud noise and smoke from neighboring land.

Nunc pro tunc

NUH'nk proh TUH'nk; NOON'k proh TOON'k

"Now for then." Refers to something that has retroactive legal effect. For example, a court's order *nunc pro tunc* applies to modify an earlier ruling from the date of that ruling.

Nuncupative will

NUN-kah-pay-tiv wil; nahn-KYOO-pah-tiv wil

An oral will. Invalid in most U.S. states. May be valid in some states with respect to certain property, and only if made in contemplation of imminent death.

O

Objection

ahb-JEK-shun

Formal expression of opposition to something in court. Parties may object to what they see as improper testimony, motions, or other actions in the case.

Objective

uhb-JEHK-tiv

Based on external and verifiable facts about the world. Objective measures stand in contrast to subjective ones, which are based on someone's intentions or perceptions.

Objectives of representation

AHB-jehk-tivs uhv rep-rez-en-TAY-shun

Main goals of a client-lawyer relationship. Picked by a client and must be obeyed by the lawyer to the extent of the law. Includes decisions on whether settle, and decisions to pick a certain criminal plea.

Obligee

ahb-lih-JEE

Anyone to whom a contractual duty is owed. Creditors and promisees may be called obligees. The person who owes a duty is called an obligor.

Obligor

AHB-lih-gor

Anyone who owes a contractual duty. Debtors and promisors may be called obligors. The person to whom a duty is owed is called an obligee.

Offer

AW-fur

A communication by someone that reasonably makes someone else think that the first person is willing to enter a contract on the terms proposed.

Offeree

AW-fer'ee

Someone to whom an offer is proposed. The person proposing the offer is called an offeror.

Offeror

AW-fer-or

Someone who makes an offer. The person to whom the offer is addressed is called an offeree.

Officer

aw-FEH'sr

In general, anyone who holds an executive position. In government, this means an elected representative or law-enforcement official. In a corporation, this means someone appointed by the board of directors to run daily business operations.

Open fields doctrine

OH-pen feeldz DAHK-trin

A rule that limits Fourth Amendment protections to one's dwelling and curtilage, but nothing beyond. For example, police may seize garbage left for collection without a warrant.

Opinion

ah-PIN-yahn

A document from a court explaining its decision on a case or disputed issue. May simply state which party won, but often goes into greater detail on the facts of the case and governing law.

Opinion testimony

ah-PIN'yun TEH-steh-moan-ee

All answers from a witness at trial except those that simply re-tell observed facts. Includes all opinions, inferences, guesses, and other subjective statements.

Option contract

AH'p-shun KAHN-trakt

Enforceable agreement to keep an offer open for a stated length of time. In the usual case, an option contract is valid because the offeree paid offeror not to revoke the offer for the time defined.

Order

OR-der

A command or instruction to someone who must obey. Most orders are written by judges, and address the parties to a dispute.

Ordinance

OR-dih-nans

An official law or government order. Most often refers to local laws. For example, a zoning ordinance might prohibit four-story houses in a residential part of town.

Organic statute

or-GAN-ik STA'tch-yoot

A legislative act that creates an administrative agency or regional government. Also called enabling statute. It grants powers and spells out limits.

Original jurisdiction

uh-REEJ-ee-nal joo-ris-DIK-shun

A court's power to be the first court that considers a certain type of dispute. For example, the U.S. Supreme Court has original jurisdiction over cases involving ambassadors.

OUI

oh yoo ai

Operating a vehicle under the influence of alcohol or other drugs. Usually a misdemeanor offense. May be a felony if serious injury results.

Output contract

AH'oot-poot KAHN-trakt

An agreement in which seller promises to sell to buyer all of a certain item or service that it manufactures or performs in a given period of time. In return, buyer promises to buy all of the relevant items or services.

Outstanding shares

out-STAN-ding SHAY'rs

The number of a corporation's shares that are actually held by investors at a given point in time. *Compare with* authorized shares, treasury stock.

Overbroad

oh-vur-BRAHD

Impacting more persons or parties than intended or allowed. A law that criminalizes more behavior than constitutionally allowed is overbroad.

Overrule

oh-ver-ROOL

(1) To reject or deny. For example, trial judges overrule objections if they disagree with them.

(2) To set aside a precedent. Courts may overrule past cases by stating that their decisions are no longer controlling law. They can also implicitly overrule cases by announcing new rules that override old ones.

Overt act

OH-vurt akt

An act that is done outwardly by physical actions. Not a mental thought. Some overt act is usually required to convict for conspiracy or attempt to commit a crime.

OWI

oh dah-b'l-yoo ai

Operating a vehicle while impaired or intoxicated by alcohol or other drugs. Usually a misdemeanor offense. May be a felony if serious injury results.

P

Paralegal

pa-rah-LEE-gahl

Someone skilled in the kind of research, case management, and paperwork required by the legal profession. Paralegals help lawyers, but are not licensed attorneys themselves.

Parol

pah-ROL

Oral. Not written. For example, a parol contract is one that is closed by word of mouth and not recorded in writing.

Parol evidence rule

pa-ROL EH-vih-dens rool

A rule that limits chances to contradict or modify written contracts. If a contract is written, and intended as a complete and final expression on a deal, then no communication before or during the time of contracting can be allowed to change the terms of the deal.

Parole

pah-ROL

Conditional release of a convicted criminal from prison before completion of the sentence. The release may be subject to conditions such as steady employment and zero drug use.

Particularity requirement

pahr-tik-yoo-LAR'ee-tee

A constitutional rule under which warrants must specifically describe places to be searched and items to be seized. The goal is ensuring a tight link between criminal suspicion and property searched.

Partnership

PART-ner-shih'p

An association of two or more people for business purposes. Partners share business profits and losses. They are either considered agents of the partnership or else joint principals.

Patent

(1) *PAT'nt*

Exclusive right to manufacture and profit from an invention during a certain period of time (e.g., 20 years). In exchange, the government obtains a full description and blueprint for later public benefit and use.

(2) *PAY-t'nt; PAT'nt;*

Extremely obvious or visible. For example, parties may sometimes get courts to revise signed contracts because of patent mistakes.

Payroll tax

PAY-rol taks

A tax that must be paid by an employer based on the number of employees it has. The cost is passed down to employees and deducted from their gross pay.

Pecuniary interest
peh-KYOO-nee-a-ree
Financial interest. Includes one's right to possess certain money, and one's ability to avoid financial liability in court.

Pen register
pen REH-jis-tur
A device that records all numbers dialed from a certain phone. More loosely, any device that performs a similar function (e.g., Internet history interceptor). May be used in police surveillance.

Per capita
pur KAP-pih-tah
(1) Per person. For example, income per capita is calculcated by dividng total income by total number of people.
(2) A law of intestacy that distributes a dead person's property by dividing it at the closest generation to the decedent with a living member. It then splits any dead taker's share among his or her heirs.

Per capita at each generation
pur KAP-pih-tah at eech jen-uh-RAY-shun
A law of intestacy that distributes a dead person's property by dividing it at the closest generation to the decedent with a living member. It then adds up shares of dead members at each level and splits them equally among heirs at the next level.

Per curiam
pur KYOO-ree-um; pur kyoo-REE-ahm
"In the opinion of the court." A byline meaning that a court with multiple judges on the panel wishes to keep secret the specific author of the opinion.

Per diem
pur DEE-ehm
"Per day." Refers to an amount of money promised to be reimbursed for every day of official duty while traveling for work.

Per quod
pur KWAH'd
"Whereby." Requiring reference to other facts, whereby something of legal significance will be established. For example, a *per quod* defamation action requires proof of some extrinsic circumstances to prove that someone was defamed.

Per se
pur say
By itself. Meaning or standing for something without further facts. For example, taking somebody's property is not unlawful per se.

Per stirpes
pur STUR-peez

A law of intestacy that distributes a dead person's property by dividing it at the closest generation to the decedent. It then splits any dead taker's share among his or her heirs.

Peremptory challenge

peh-REMP-to-ree CHA-len'j

A party's request to dismiss someone from a jury panel, when no reason to dmiss is given. Each party in a case has a limited number of such challenges. Also called peremptory strike.

Perfect tender rule

PUR-fekt TEN-dur rool

The right to reject goods if they fail to conform to the contract, even if no material breach occurs. The Uniform Commercial Code includes this rule.

Perfection

pur-FEK-shun

The taking of legal steps necessary to preserve a claim or right. For example, security interests are usually perfected only if creditors file public notices.

Periodic estate

pee-ree-AH-dik eh-STAY't

A type of lease set to continue for repeated and fixed segments of time. Examples include weekly, monthly, or yearly periods. Ends only when notice is given in accordance with a contract.

Perjury

PUR-joo-ree

Lying under oath about a material fact. The statement must be deliberate, and either false or misleading. Material means legally relevant to the proceedings where made.

Personal deductions

pur-SUN-ahl dee-DUK-shuns

Deductions from taxable income that are supposed to reflect the cost of basic survival. U.S. federal taxpayers can either itemize specific deductions or subtract a standard deduction amount.

Personal injury

PUR-so-nahl IN-jyoo-ree

A harm to one's body. Includes physical as well as psychological harm. Can also mean an impairment of rights that is personal to the plaintiff and nobody else.

Personal jurisdiction

PUR-sah-nahl joo-ris-DIK-shun

A court's power over the parties to a dispute. Without power over one's personal rights and interests, there can be no binding judgment against them. Also called *in personam* jurisdiction.

Personal representative

PUR-so-nahl rep-reh-ZEN-(t)uh-tiv

A person with authority over a deceased person's property. If appointed under a will, called an executor. If appointed by a court in cases of intestacy, called an administrator.

Perspective bias

pur-SPEH'k-tiv BAH-yus

A tendency to overestimate the likelihood that one's position is correct. An understanding of perspective biases is important to resolving disputes.

Persuasive authority

pur-SWAY-siv uh-THO-reh-tee

Legal precedents that are not binding on the court deciding a case. Includes decisions from this court itself, lower courts, and higher courts of other jursdictions.

Petitioner

peh-TIH-shuh-nur

A party that files an official request in court. May refer to the plaintiff, but also to a defendant who brings an appeal to a higher court.

Photo identification

FOE-tow ai-den-teh-fih-KAY-shun

(1) A card or other document that verifies identity. Commonly called photo ID. Examples include a driver's license, and a college identification card with the student's photo.

(2) A "virtual" lineup in which a victim or witness is given photographs, and asked if any of the people pictured committed the crime. Also called a photo array.

Piercing the corporate veil

PEER-sing thuh kor-po-RUT VEY'il

A legal remedy by which courts strip away the limited liability of a corporation and make one or more of its owners personally liable for its debts. Used only in clear cases of foul play by the owners.

Piracy

PAI-ruh-see

(1) Unlawful copying or distribution of intellectual property. Includes material that is patented, copyrighted, or trademarked.
(2) Unlawful violence committed at sea. Includes robberies and kidnappings for ransom.

Plain meaning rule

PLAY'n MEE-ning rool

An idea that courts must apply statutes that are clear and constitutional, even if the result seems absurd in a given case.

Plain view

PLAY'n vyoo

One exception to the Fourth Amendment's general warrant requirement. Warrantless seizures are permitted if police have a right to be somewhere, see something in plain sight, and have probable cause to believe it is evidence of a crime.

Plaintiff

PLAY'n-tif

The party that files a lawsuit. May be a person or entity, such as a corporation or government. Also called claimant or complainant.

Plea

plee

The formal answer to criminal charges made by a criminal defendant in court. The most common pleas are "guilty," "not guilty," and "no contest."

Plea bargain

plee BAR-gun

An agreement between a criminal defendant and prosecutor. The defendant may plead guilty to a lesser charge, or just one of many charges. The prosecutor may drop some charges or ask for a softer punishment.

Pleading

PLEE-ding

A document filed in court, through which a party raises claims, defenses, motions, and objections. Examples include the plaintiff's complaint and the defendant's answer.

Poison pill

POY-zun pil

Defensive scheme used to prevent hostile takeover of a corporation. Usually lets shareholders buy many shares at a discount if a single party acquires a large percentage of stock. This dilutes the hostile stockholder's voting power. Also called a shareholder rights plan.

Political question

puh-LIT-ih-kahl KWES-chun

An issue that involves discretionary decisions by legislative or executive officials. Courts cannot review such issues because no sufficient standards exist.

Possibility of reverter

pah-si-BIL-eh-tee uhv ree-VUR-tur

Future interest in property that remains with the grantor after he or she grants a fee simple determinable to someone. Automatically ends fee simple determinable if a stated event occurs.

Power

PAH-u'r

In general, the ability to act or decline to act. In contracts, the ability to act in a way that alters legal duties. Since the power to act is not the same as the right to act, the acting party may be liable for breach.

Power of attorney

PAU-er uhv uh-TUR-nee

A document in which one designates an agent to act and make decisions in his or her place. Also the name for authority so granted.

Precatory

PREH-kah-to-ree

Urging action or expressing wishes, but not clearly causing legally binding results. For example, the phrase "I hope he takes care of her," is precatory language.

Precedent
(1) PREH-seh-dent

An official decision made in the past. Judicial precedents serve as guidance for deciding new cases in court. Sometimes, the guidance is merely persuasive (may be consulted), and sometimes mandatory (must be applied).

(2) preh-SEE-dent

Prior; taking place before something else. Thus, a condition precedent is an event that must occur before contractual duties are due to be performed.

Preexisting duty
pree-eg-ZIS-ting DYU-tee

A duty that someone is already obligated to perform. Promising to perform a preexisting duty cannot serve as valid consideration for a new contract.

Preferential payment
pre-feh-REN-shul TREE't-ment

A transfer of property by a debtor shortly before declaring bankruptcy. A typical period is 90 days in advance. Courts may order such property back into the bankruptcy estate.

Preferred stock
pree-FURD STAH'k

A type of ownership share in a corporation that does not always have voting rights, but always receives a stated dividend if dividends are distributed. In the case of liquidation, preferred stockholders get paid before any common stockholders.

Preliminary injunction
pree-LIM-eeh-nary in-JUNK-shun

An injunction of temporary effect, issued during the start or middle of trial. The goal is to preserve the status quo before final judgment on the merits. Advance notice to the opposing party is required.

Preponderance of the evidence
pree-PAHN-deh-rans uhv thuh EH-vih-dens

The majority of the evidence, measured in persuasive strength and not number of items. In civil cases, questions of fact generally must be proven only by a preponderance of the evidence.

Presumption rule
preh-ZAHM'p-shun rool

A requirement that a particular inference be accepted as the truth if a given set of facts is proven. Some presumptions leave a chance for rebuttal, but others do not.

Pretermitted
pree-tur-MIH-ted

Overlooked or ignored. May be intentional or accidental. For example, pretermitted heirs are children or spouses omitted from someone's will.

Pretext

PREE-tek'st

A stated motive that is actually false or weak compared to the real motive. Police sometimes use pretextual arrests or searches to look for evidence of another crime.

Pretrial conference

PREE- trai-yul KAHN-feh-rens

Relatively informal meeting between a judge and attorneys for the parties. Held before trial to discuss evidence matters, general deadlines, and the possibility of settling the case.

Prima facie

PREE-mah FAY-shuh; PREE-mah FAY-shee

First view. The elements that must be alleged to create a legal presumption. Without a valid defense or rebuttal, that presumption becomes the truth. Prima facie elements differ for each crime and tort.

Primary jurisdiction doctrine

PRAI-maree joo-ris-DIK-shun DAHK-trin

A requirement that administrative agencies must be the first to decide matters within their competence. Courts involved too soon in the process should dismiss the case.

Principal

PRIN-sih-pul

Someone who authorizes another person to act in his or her place. The person representing a principal is called an agent.

Principal in the first degree

PRIN-sih-pal in thuh furst deh-GREE

A main or substantial actor who actually commits a crime. Not someone who is just criminally liable as an accomplice.

Principal in the second degree

PRIN-sih-pal in thuh SEK-und deh-GREE

Someone who helps commit a crime and is actually present at the crime scene. *Compare with* accessory.

Prior art

PRAH-yor akt

In patent law, a general term that includes all public knowledge and inventions in a given field. Inventions falling within prior art cannot be patented.

Prior restraint

PRAH-yer reh-STRAY'int

Government restriction on speech before it is actually expressed. The U.S. Constitution's First Amendment generally makes prior restraint unlawful.

Priority

prah-YOH-rih-tee

Description for something that came earlier or is otherwise more important. In secured transactions, priority rules determine the order in which creditors take cash from property that is sold to satisfy debts.

Prisoner's dilemma
prih-ZAH-nurs dih-LEH-mah
Famous explanation for why two parties might not cooperate despite it being in their best interests. The problem stems from inadequate information and communcation.

Private nuisance
PRAI-vet NYOO-sens
An activity or condition that infinges on a person's right to use and enjoy property, without affecting the general public. One example is explosions that shake a neighbor's house.

Privilege
PRIH-vih-lej
A right to do or refuse to do something. Examples include the right to use force in self-defense, and the right not to testify against oneself.

Privileges and Immunities Clause
PRIH-vil-eh-jez and i-MUYN-ities klawz
Article IV, Section 1 of the U.S. Constitution. It prohibits fundamental discrimination against state citizens who travel to another state.

Privity
PRIH-veh-tee
Any non-hostile connection between different people. Contractual privity refers to parties who agreed to a deal by contract. Privity of estate refers to joint or successive interests in the same property.

Pro bono
pro BOW-no
Shortened version of *pro bono publico* ("for the public good"). The act of providing uncompensated legal services, or the name for such services themselves.

Pro se
pro say
For oneself. A party acting without an attorney in court is said to be proceeding or acting *pro se*. Organizations exist to help such people navigate the law.

Probable cause
PRAH-bah'bl kawz
Reasonably trustworthy information, based on specific facts, that is sufficient to convince a prudent and cautious person that a crime has been committed, and possibly that a certain person committed it.

Probate
PRO-bayt
(1) Relating to the distribution of one's property after death. Probate courts are specifically created to handle such matters, either under a will or laws of intestacy.
(2) The act of granting probation to someone convicted of a crime.

Probation

proh-BAY-shun

A criminal sentence that lets defendants stay out of jail if they follow stated conditions for a certain period of time. Steady employment and zero drug use are possible conditions.

Procedural due process

prah-SEE-dyu-rahl dyu PRAH-ses

A requirement that government procedures must be fair to the persons affected. Thus, notice and hearing must be given before limiting one's right to life, liberty, or property.

Production

prah-DUHK-shun

Act of making something available, usually to the opposing party in a case. Documents and witnesses may be said to be produced when they are made available for examination.

Products liability

PRAH-duh'kts lah-yah-BIH-leh-tee

A way to hold manufacturers and sellers accountable for defective goods. Buyers, consumers, or mere bystanders may sue for injuries due to defects in manufacture or design.

Profit

PRAH-fit

(1) The difference between money acquired and the cost to acquire that money. In other words, revenues minus expenditures.

(2) A limited right to take soil or products of the soil from from someone else's land. May include timber, minerals, and oil.

Progressive tax

prah-GREH-siv taks

A tax that charges a lower percentage on initially-acquired property, and gradually higher percentages on property acquired later by the same person in a period of time.

Promise

PRAH-mihs

Expression of intent to do or not do something. A gratuitous promise (made as a gift with no value in exchange) does not create an enforceable contract.

Promisee

prah-mih-SEE

Someone to whom a promise is made. The person making a promise is called a promisor.

Promisor

PRAH-mihs-or

Someone who makes a promise. The person to whom a promise is made is called a promisee.

Promissory estoppel

PRAH-mi-soh-ree eh-STAH'pl

The enforcement of a promise despite the lack of consideration or valid contract. Applies when the promisor should reasonably know that someone could rely on his promise and such reliance occurs.

Promoter
pruh-MOW-ter

A business entity's organizer or creator. Promoters are the people who think of creating a business organization and submit the paperwork required to do so.

Promoter liability
pruh-MOW-ter lah-yah-BIH-leh-tee

Personal liability that may be imposed on the creators of a new business. Promoters are personally liable for debts assumed on behalf of a corporation before the corporation had legal existence.

Proof of claim
proof uhv KLAY'm

A document filed by a creditor in bankruptcy court to establish its claim to a debtor's property. Should list the value owed and how the debt arose.

Property tax
PRAH-pur-tee taks

A tax that must be paid by property owners. Most often applied to real property only, and calculated from its assessed value.

Prosecutor
PRAH-see-kyoo-tor

A government lawyer who represents the general public in cases against criminal defendants.

Prospective client
PRAH-spek-tiv KLAI-yent

A person who seeks professional services. Lawyers owe prospective clients a duty of confidentiality even if no attorney-client relationship results.

Protected class
prah-TEHK-ted klas

Group of people that a law aims to protect. Examples include the underage or the handicapped. The victim's consent may be no defense if the victim was part of a relevant protected class.

Protective trust
prah-TEK-tiv truh'st

A category of trusts created with the goal of carefully supporting the beneficiary in life. The trustee is given full or significant discretion over when to pay out trust property to the beneficiary.

Proximate cause
PRAH'k-si-maht kawz

An actual cause that was so close to the injury in time and space that it will make someone liable. A criminal's parents are actual causes of the crime, but are not proximate causes and thus not liable by virtue of being parents.

Proxy vote

PRAH'ksee voat

A vote by someone who is not actually present at the meeting where voting occurs. Instead, the voter authorizes someone else to vote in his or her place.

Public corporation

PUB-lik kor-puh-RAY-shun

(1) A corporation with publicly traded shares. Anyone with the funds to buy at least one share can become one of the owners.

(2) A corporation that is owned or backed by the government. Its activities are typically meant to benefit the general public.

Public defender

PUB-lik deh-FEN-der

An attorney appointed to represent someone at public expense. The goal is to ensure justice for all persons and not just for the wealthy or powerful.

Public disclosure of private facts

PUB-lik dis-KLOW-zhur uhv PRAI-vet fakt's

Publicizing private information or private images of someone. Must be objectionable to a reasonable person. Usually needs to be disclosed to a sizeable group of people to be unlawful.

Public domain

PUB-lik doh-MAY'n

(1) Set of all knowledge, inventions, and expressions that are not within anyone's intellectual property rights. Such items can be used and reproduced without anyone's authorization.

(2) Land owned by the government. Historically, referred most often to land owned by the U.S. federal government.

Public forum

PUB-lik FOR-um

A place traditionally used to share speech. Public parks, sidewalks, and street corners are public forums. School auditoriums and city meeting halls are more limited public forums.

Public nuisance

PUB-lik NYOO-sens

An activity or condition that infringes on some right of the general public. Examples include toxic fumes and unlawfully blocking a street.

Public policy

PUB-lik PAH-leh-see

General principles that are important to the public. May be inferred from statutes and judicial decisions. Public policy can make some contracts unenforceable.

Publication

pub-li-KAY-shun

An element needed to prove defamation. Requires communication of the defamatory statement to a third person who understood what it meant.

Pullman abstention
PUL-mahn ab-STEHN-shun
A way for U.S. federal courts to decline cases that involve centrally important and unsettled questions of state law. This allows a state court to handle the dispute.

Punitive damages
PYOO-neh-tiv DAM-eh-jes
Money awarded on top of actual damages suffered. The usual goal is to prevent the wrongdoer from repeating its actions by making them more expensive. Also called exemplary damages.

Purchase money security interest (PMSI)
PUR-ches MAH-nee seh-KYOO-rih-tee INT-rest (pee em ehs ai)
A security interest in some item that a buyer gives to a creditor, after the creditor lends money so that buyer can buy that specific item. *See* security interest.

Purposeful availment
PUR-pus-ful
Deliberate use and enjoyment. When checking for minimum contacts for purposes of personal jurisdiction, courts may ask whether a party purposefully availed itself of the privilege of conducting business in the state where the court sits.

Purposely
PUR-pus-lee
Doing something with the conscious and deliberate intention to do it or cause some result.

Put option
poot AH'p-shun
A contract that allows one party to sell something to another party for a fixed price within a certain time. Used in trading to hedge against price drops.

Q

Quantum meruit

KWAH'n-tum MEH-roo-it

"As much as earned." The reasonable value of services provided or goods transferred. In an action for unjust enrichment, this is the measure of damages.

Quash

kw'AH-sh

To cancel out, suppress, or terminate. For example, a motion to quash to a subpoena may be made if the wrong person is identified in the subpoena.

Quasi in rem jurisdiction

KWAZ-ai in rehm joo-ris-DIK-shun

A court's power to decide the rights of competing parties to the same piece of property. The issues considered need not always be related to that property.

Quasi-contract

KWAZ-ai KAHN-trakt

A performance or promise that is insufficient to form a contract, but still recognized to some extent in court. Unjust enrichment and promissory estoppel are the main theories involved.

Quasi-suspect classification

KWAZ-ai SUS-pekt CLAS-ih-feh-kay-shun

Statutory discrimination based on gender or the legitimacy of a child. Quasi-suspect classifications usually need to pass intermediate scrutiny.

Question of fact

KWES-chun uhv fakt

An issue that centers on whether, when, where, how, or why certain events happened. Also called issue or matter of fact. *Compare with* question of law.

Question of law

KWES-chun uhv law

An issue that centers on the meaning of a certain law, how it is affected by other laws, and how it should be applied to facts. Also called issue or matter of law. *Compare with* question of fact.

Quitclaim deed

KWIT- klay'm dee'd

A document that transfers whatever interest the grantor has in certain property, if any. It does not promise that grantor had valid title without defects.

Quorum

KWO-rum

Minimum number of eligible people who must attend a meeting so that binding decisions can be made at that meeting. Most legislative bodies and corporations set quorums for their meetings.

R

Race statute

ray's STA'tch-yoot

A recording act that resolves ownership disputes by giving title to whichever party records his or her purchase first. Even a party with actual notice of prior sale can win title by recording first.

Race-notice statute

ray's NO-tis STA'tch-yoot

A recording act that gives title to a later good-faith buyer rather than an earlier buyer who failed to record the purchase, but only if the later buyer records first.

Rape

RAY'p

Unlawful sexual intercourse with a person, other than a spouse, without that person's valid consent. Victims are more commonly female than male.

Rational basis review

REH-shun-ul BAY-sis reh-VYU

A test asking whether government action is rationally related to a legitimate government purpose. A law properly subjected to this test and found lacking is invalid.

Real property

reel PRAH-per-tee

Land, anything growing or built on land, and rights (such as easements) that are connected to the use of land. Also called realty.

Realization

ree-ah-liz-AE-shun

Clear change in someone's financial position. The time at which a gain or loss occurs. For example, a sale of stock for cash is a realization event.

Reasonable

REE-zah-nuh'bl

Fair, prudent, or proper given the situation. Driving 60 miles per hour on a freeway is usually reasonable. Driving 60 miles per hour next to a school is not.

Reasonable

REE-zun-aw'bl

Fair, moderate, and proper. Many legal rules ask how a reasonable person would have acted under the circumstances of a dispute.

Reasonable person

REE-zah-nuh'bl PUR'sn

Hypothetical benchmark for lawful action. This "person" has average mental ability and knowledge, but the same physical characteristics as the individual whose actions are being questioned.

Rebuttable
ree-BUH-tah-b'l
Capable of being disputed and disproven. Unlike an argument that is conclusive, an argument that is rebuttable is open to new facts, questions, and changes.

Rebuttal
ree-BUH-tel
An argument or conclusive proof that something is not true. In legal disputes, some claims need to be rebutted in a certain amount of time, or else the initial claim is accepted as the truth.

Recklessly
REK-les-lee
Doing something while consciously disregarding a substantial or unjustifiable risk of injury. Reckless actions fall grossly short of a relevant standard of care.

Record
REH-kord
A written account of past events. Trial courts and administrative agencies often compile records of proceedings. These records are crucial for judicial review.

Record owner
REH-kord OWN-ur
Someone whose name appears on a legal title, but who holds the property in trust for another party. The other party has rights to sell or enjoy the property. *See* beneficial owner.

Recording act
reh-KOR-ding akt
A law that requires buyers of property to record their purchases in a public place to put third parties on notice. Failure to record might give a different *bona fide* purchaser title to the property.

Recovery
ree-KAH-veh-ree
The regaining or retaking of something. In court, recovery refers to compensation that is awarded for an injury. *See, e.g.,* damages.

Redemption
reh-DEMP-shun
The retaking or reclaiming of something. For example, homeowners in foreclosure may redeem their rights in a house by paying all their debts to a lender.

Reduction to practice
ree-DUK-shun too PRAK-tis
Proof that an invention can actually work as claimed. Reduction may be actual (physically made or carried out), or constructive (sufficiently explained and diagrammed).

Regressive tax

ree-GREH-siv taks

A tax that charges a higher percentage on initially-acquired property, and gradually lower percentages on property acquired later by the same person in a period of time.

Release

ree-LEES

Voluntary surrender of a right to sue somebody for one or more of that person's actions. For example, plaintiffs might release one of multiple defendants from a lawsuit in exchange for money.

Relevant

REH-leh-vent

Logically related to a question, and making at least one answer to that question more or less likely to be true. Even a tiny impact on likelihood can make something relevant.

Reliance damages

reh-LAI-yun's DAM-eh-jes

Money awarded to compensate a contracting party for losses due to reasonable reliance on the contract. The amount should return the contracting party to its financial position before the contract arose.

Relief

REH-leef

Help given to people in need. In court, this refers to damages or other benefits awarded to parties who suffered an injury. Also called remedy.

Remainder

ree-MAY'n-der

A future interest in property. May be held by any person (even those not yet born), except the initial creator of the estate, its first holder, and the heirs of either one.

Remainder beneficiary

ree-MAY'n-der beh-neh-FIH-shuh-ree

Someone who may or must receive assets from the final distribution of a trust. Unlike an income beneficiary, worries more about aggressive investments.

Remittitur

reh-MH-tih-tur

The grant of a new trial, or an award of damages lower than the amount awarded by a jury – requiring plaintiff to choose between the two.

Removal

ree-MOOV-ahl

Transfer of a case from one court to another. In the U.S., defendants may sometimes take cases originally filed in state court and remove them to a federal court.

Reorganization
REE-or-gah-nih-ZAY-shun

Change in setup. In bankruptcy law, a change in who owns rights to an income stream, and what portion they own. Courts may reorganize a corporation's business or an individual's wages.

Replevin
rep-LEH-vin

Judicial action in which plaintiff sues to recover property that was allegedly wrongly taken by defendant. Courts may immediately transfer the property to plaintiff, before eventually deciding who owns it.

Repurchase
ree-PUR-chus

Buying something back that belonged to the buyer in the past. Outstanding shares repurchased by a corporation become known as treasury stock.

Request for admission
ree-KWEST for uhd-MIH-shun

A statement of fact sent to an opposing party in a case. The opposing party must admit, deny, or object to the statement. Admitted or ignored statements are established as true for the case.

Requirements contract
ree-KWA-yer-ments KAHN-trakt

An agreement in which buyer promises to buy from seller all of a certain item or service that it needs during a given period of time. In return, seller promises to supply the required amount.

Res
REH'z

A thing or piece of property. For example, the property placed in a trust for management by the trustee may either be called a corpus or a res.

Res gestae
rez JEZ-tai

"Things done." The events giving rise a crime or legal dispute, and other events that were occurring at the same time.

Res ipsa loquitur
rez IP-sah LAHK-wih-tur

"Thing speaks for itself." A rule that helps some plaintiffs prove a breach of duty in tort claims. Injuries that do not typically occur without negligence raise an inference that whoever was in control was likely negligent.

Res judicata
rez joo-dih-KAH-tah

An adjudicated thing. Something that has already been decided in court and need not be proven again. *See* claim preclusion, collateral estoppel.

Rescission
reh-SIH-zhun

Contracting parties' agreement to cancel their contract, or a unilateral cancellation by one party for a legally sufficient reason.

Residue
REH-zih-dyoo
Something that is left after essential parts are gone. In a will, residue includes all property that is not expressly devised to someone. The will may identify a residuary taker, or such property may be distributed under laws of intestacy.

Respondeat superior
ree-SPON-dee-at soo-PEE-ree-or
"Let the superior answer." A common form of vicarious liability. It forces employers to compensate some people injured by their employees.

Respondent
res-PAHN-dent
A party that opposes an official request in court. May refer to the defendant, but also a plaintiff who defends a winning verdict on appeal.

Restatement
ree-STAY't-ment
A summary of existing rules on a given subject of law. Published by the American Law Institute, Restatements generally reflect legal rules that are in effect in a majority states.

Restitution
res-tee-TYOO-shun
(1) Compensation for property damage or the restoration of something to its rightful owner.
(2) A type of liability that comes from a need to prevent unjust enrichment. Restitution damages are based on the amount of defendant's unfair gain, which may well differ from the amount of plaintiff's loss.

Resulting trust
ree-ZUH'l-ting truh'st
A trust that may be recognized in court, as long as an intent to create a trust existed even though it was not actually or validly expressed.

Retainer
ree-TAY-nur
An agreement between a lawyer and client authorizing the lawyer to act in the client's interests. Can also refer to money paid by client to lawyer to ensure the lawyer's availability to work on a matter.

Reverse
ree-VIRS
To reject or overturn. Appellate courts may reverse decisions of lower courts for mistakes. After reversal, the lower court can either redo a step, or issue an order giving effect to the higher court's conclusions.

Reversion
ree-VUR-zhun

Future interest in property that remains with the grantor after he or she grants an estate of shorter time length than he or she has.

Revocation

reh-voh-CAY-shun

In general, any cancellation or withdrawal. In contracts, the withdrawal of an offer. In wills and estates, someone's invalidation of his or her will, either by cancellation or replacement.

Right

ruy't

In general, anything that is legally proper or guaranteed. In constitutional law, a choice or claim protected by law. In contracts, the right to take an action insultates the acting party from liability for breach.

Right to counsel

ruy't too KAUN-sel

A right to be represented by a lawyer, possibly at public expense. The U.S. Constitution protects this right at various stages of criminal interrogation and trial.

Riparian rights

rai-PA-ree-un ruy'ts

The rights of someone with property next to a river or stream to use water from it. Such rights may be detached and sold separately from the right to possess land.

Ripeness

RUYP-nes

In a dispute, the development of facts to a point at which a judicial decision can be intelligently made. Hypothetical worries without imminent injury are not enough.

Robbery

RAH-ber-ree

Taking another's personal property by force or threats, from the owner or in the owner's presence. Requires an intent to perrmanently keep it from the owner.

Roe v. Wade

row vee weyd

Decision of the U.S. Supreme Court that prohibits outright bans on abortion. The decision stemmed from a woman's right to privacy. It allowed increasingly more state regulation during the course of a woman's pregnancy.

Rule

rool

(1) A general standard or principle. Legal rules help ensure that similar facts receive similar treatment under the laws.

(2) A regulation enacted by an administrative agency. Such rules often take legislative statutes and convert them into concrete standards.

Rule against perpetuities (RAP)

rool ah-GEH'nst pur-pah-TYOO-ih-tees

A requirement that wipes out certain distant future interests in property. Contingent future interests are invalid if they might vest more than 21 years after the death of a relevant person. This old rule has been modified in many states.

Rule in Shelley's case

rool in SHEH-leez kaes

A property law rule that effectively gives a fee simple absolute to a person if a single grant gives a freehold estate to that person and the remainder to that person's heirs.

Rule of lenity

rool uhv LEH-nee-tee

A requirement that ambiguous criminal statutes must be applied strictly in favor of the defendant. Thus, if two interpretations are reasonable, the one less harsh to the defendant must be applied.

Rulemaking

ROOL-may-king

The process by which administrative agencies make or modify rules. It usually involves notice to the public and some time to revise the initially proposed rule.

S

Safe harbor

SAY'if HAHR-bur

A type of provision inserted into laws to protect technical violators from liability. The ususal goal is to protect good-faith actors from punishment for relatively minor violations.

Sales tax

SAY'ilz taks

A charge by the government that is based on sales of property or services. Usually calculated as a percentage of sales price.

Sarbanes–Oxley Act

SAR-bay'ns AH'ks-lee akt

U.S. federal law passed in response to corporate accounting scandals of the early 2000s. It imposed stricter rules on financial disclosures by publicly traded companies.

Satisfaction

sa-tis-FAK-shun

Value given to pay a debt in full. For example, a plaintiff who sues multiple defendants for one injury cannot recover more money than needed to satisfy awarded damages.

Saving provision

SAY-ving PRAH-vee-zhun

Words in a new statute that tell courts to judge actions committed before this statute by then-existing laws on the same topic.

Scienter

see-EN-tur

Sufficient degree of knowledge to make one liable for something such as fraud. Requires knowledge that something was false, or at least reckless disregard to its truth or falsity.

Scintilla

sin-TIH-lah

A mere spark or shred of evidence. Some legal rules allow a scintilla standard of proof. Others require more than a mere scintilla of evidence.

Search

SUR'ch

(1) Examination of a person's body or property in hopes of finding evidence of a crime. To get Fourth Amendment protection, one must have a reasonable expectation of privacy in the area searched.

(2) Examination of public records. The usual goal is to protect one's rights. For example, a title search may reveal that the seller of a house actually has no rights in that property.

Search incident to lawful arrest

SUR'ch IN-sih-dent too LAW-ful AH-rest

One exception to the Fourth Amendment's general warrant requirement. If police have probable cause to arrest someone, they may search that person and nearby property without a warrant.

Second Amendment

SEK-und

Second Amendment of the U.S. Constitution. Protects an individual's right to keep a firearm. The right originally stemmed from the need to prevent tyranny through militias.

Second degree murder

SEK-und deh-GREE MUR-der

Initial degree of any murder in states that use a degree system for murder. Becomes a first degree murder if aggravated by factors such as cool premeditation and occurrence during another violent felony.

Secured

seh-KYOO'rd

Descriptive term for any obligation supported by collateral or other type of interest in property. Loans backed by security interests are called secured loans. Creditors who give secured loans are called secured creditors or parties.

Securities

se-KYOO-ri-ties

Documents that prove ownership rights in a firm (such as shares) or rights to the repayment of debt (such as bonds). Securities trading usually needs careful regulation to prevent manipulation or fraud.

Securities and Exchange Commission (SEC)

se-KYOO-ri-ties and eks-CHANJ ka-MISH-un (ess ee see)

U.S. federal agency that regulates securities trading. Typically checks for insider trading and fraud in the financial reports of corporations.

Security interest

seh-KYOO-rih-tee INT-rest

A limited interest in property given by its owner to someone else. As specified by agreement, that limited interest can turn into full-fledged ownership if the present owner fails to perform some obligation.

Seduction

SEH-duck-shun

Non-forceful persuasion by a man of a woman, ending with unlawful sexual relations between the two. The woman needs to have a previously chaste reputation. Usually no longer a crime.

Seizure

SEE-zhur

The taking into custody of a person or thing by some claimed legal right. Includes all confiscation of property and arrests by law enforcement officials.

Self-defense

seh'lf deh-FENS

Use of force to pretect oneself. Reasonable force is generally allowed to protect oneself from reasonably expected imminent bodily harm.

Sentence

SEN-tens

The punishment given to a convicted criminal defendant. May include prison time, probation, restitution, and community service.

Sentence enhancement

SEN-tens en-HANS-ment

The practice of increasing criminal punishment because the convicted criminal defendant has been convicted of other crimes in the past.

Separation of church and state

SEP-uh-ray-shun uhv chur-ch and stayt

The idea that government should not be allowed to entangle itself with any organized religion, and vice-versa.

Separation of powers

sep-uh-RAY-shun uhv PAH-wurs

Division of government into multiple branches (e.g., legislative, executive, judicial). The goal is to create checks and balances, and to prevent tyranny.

Sequestration

see-kwe-STRAY-shun

(1) Official isolation of someone during trial. Jurors may be sent to an undisclosed hotel to prevent tampering by journalists. Witnesses may be kept out of the courtroom so they do not copy the testimony of others.

(2) Official seizure of property, usually by a court. For example, property may be sequestered after default judgment, or held until a true owner is found.

Service of process

SUR-vis uhv PRAH-ses

The formal delivery of a complaint and court summons to a defendant. May be delivered in person by a non-party in the case, or through other ways such as mail.

Settlement

SEH-tel-ment

(1) An agreement ending a legal dispute. Typically, plaintiff stops the lawsuit in exchange for defendant's payment of money.

(2) Final payment or disposition of debts. For example, a dissolving corporation should settle all of its accounts.

(3) Voluntary distribution of property to one's beneficiaries. May refer to distribution under a will, or distribution during the owner's life that differs from what the beneficiaries would receive as heirs upon death.

Settlor

SET'lur

The person who creates a trust. Typically, must express an intent to create a trust, and place the first trust property under the trustee's control.

Several liability
SEH-veh-rahl lah-yah-BIH-leh-tee
The responsibility of a party only for his or her share of an obligation. For example, a judgment of several liability prevents plaintiff from recovering the full amount of damages from one party. *Compare with* joint and several liability.

Severance
SEH-veh-rens
Split or division. For example, a joint tenancy may be severed if the owners no longer want to hold property together. A severance payment may be made when a worker leaves a company.

Shareholder
SHAY'r-hol-der
Someone who owns shares in a corporation, or for whose beneficial use someone else holds the shares. *See* beneficial owner, record owner.

Shipment contract
SHIP-ment KAHN-trakt
A deal in which seller is responsible for risk of loss or damage to goods only until their delivery to a shipper. *Compare with* destination contract.

Shopkeeper's privilege
SHAH'p-kee-purs PRIH-vi-leh'dj
A possible defense to claims of false imprisonment. Allows store workers to detain suspected thieves for a reasonable time and in a reasonable manner for investigation.

Signature
SIG-nah-chur
A name or mark written by someone to authenticate a document. Can be physically written by someone else at the signing party's direction.

Situs
SAI-toos
Location or place. For example, the *situs* of a contract is the place where it was executed.

Sixth Amendment
SIH'ks'th uh-MEND-ment
Sixth Amendment of the U.S. Constitution. It protects rights to a speedy trial and to confront witnesses. In many cases, also guarantees a jury and a publicly funded attorney.

Slayer statute
SLA-yer STATCH-yoot
A law that bars inheritance by will or intestacy for people who intentionally or feloniously caused the deceased person to die.

Solicitation

sah-lih-sih-TAY-shun

(1) Asking or commanding another to commit a crime. To be convicted of solicitation, the defendant must have had a specific intent for the other person to actually commit the crime.

(2) Loosely, asking for anything. A "no solicitation" sign on a house means that salespeople and others are not authorized on the property without a legal right.

Special agent

speh-SHUL AY-jent

(1) In criminal law, a common title given to investigative law enforcement officials.

(2) In agency law, someone authorized to represent the principal in a single transaction only, or else in a chain of transactions over some period of time.

Specific intent

speh-SIH-fik in-TENT

A mental state in which someone acts with a certain goal in mind. For example, larceny requires a specific intent to deprive an owner of his property.

Specific jurisdiction

speh-SIH-fik joo-ris-DIK-shun

Specific personal jurisdiction. A court's power over a party that only allows it to hear disputes specifically connected to whatever activity serves as the basis for personal jursidiction.

Specific performance

speh-SIH-fik pehr-FOR-muns

A judicial remedy, based on the law of equity, that directs someone to perform specific action rather than pay money damages. Specific performance is often ordered if one party breaches a real-estate sales contract.

Specific tax

speh-SIH-fik taks

A tax according to quantity. A fixed sum based on the number of items in a certain category, regardless of each item's market value.

Speedy trial

SPEE-dee TRAI-yul

A trial of proper length for balancing the interests of the public and the defendant. The U.S. Constitution's Sixth Amendment protects a right to speedy trial. If delays occur, factors to consider include the length and reason for delay, prejudice to the defendant, and possible waiver of the right.

Spendthrift trust

SPEND-thrift truh'st

A protective trust with the main goal of preventing careless decisions by the beneficiary. It does not allow beneficiaries to transfer their interest in the trust, and creditors cannot seize the beneficiary's interest.

Standard of care

STAN-durd uhv KAY'r

Level of caution required in a given situation. In general, everyone must act towards others as would an ordinary, reasonable, and prudent person. Other standards exist, often based one one's status or profession.

Standard of review

STAN-durd uhv reh-VYU

The test by which a court checks the validity of government action or the correctness of another court's decision. Different cases require different standards of review.

Standing

STAN-ding

Plaintiff's significant stake in a dispute. Standing requires actual or imminent injury, causation running to defendant, and the court's ability to offer relief.

Stare decisis

STA-ree de-SAI-sis

"Stand by decided things." A principle that obligates judges to consult and often be bound by past judicial holdings.

State action

stayt AK-shun

Action committed by the government, or a private party closely entangled with the government, or a private party whose action is only effective because judicially enforced.

Statement against interest

STAY't ah-GEH'nst INT-rest

A statement that ran counter to a person's interest when the person made it. The interest may be related to criminal punishment, money, or other property. Usually an exception to hearsay rules.

Statute

STA'tch-yoot

A law passed by a legislature. Must pass all constitutional tests to be valid. Often complicated if it regulates activity with great detail and precision.

Statute of frauds

STA'tch-yoot uhv fraw'dz

A rule that prevents enforcement of some contracts unless they are written. Includes contracts for $500 or more in sales, contracts for land sales, and contracts incapable of performance within one year.

Statute of limitations
STA'tch-yoot uhv li-mi-TAY-shuns
Specified period during which a claim or criminal charge must be filed. It starts when wrongdoing occurred, or when its result should have been discovered.

Statutory rape
STA'tch-yoo-toh-ree RAY'p
Sexual intercourse with a person who is legally too young to give valid consent. Typically, only adults are convicted of statutory rape.

Stay
sta'y
Official pause to judicial proceedings or to the rights of creditors to demand repayment of debt. Some things that are stayed end up permanently suspended.

Stock
STAH'k
(1) Money raised by a corporation from the sale of shares. Also the name for those shares themselves.
(2) Goods stored by a merchant for sale or trade.

Stop and frisk
STAH'p and frih'sk
A warrantless search of a person in public. Constitutional if it rests on articulable and reasonable suspicion of criminal activity in the area. The person may be searched for weapons if reasonably believed to be armed and dangerous. Also known as a *Terry* stop or investigatory detention.

Strict liability
strikt lah-yah-BIH-leh-tee
Guilt for a crime, or liability for a tort, that does not require fault. In other words, the defendant need not have intended the unlawful action, or known about any risk.

Strict scrutiny
strikt SKROO-t'nee
A test asking whether government action is necessary and narrowly tailored to achieve a compelling government purpose. A law properly subjected to this test and found lacking is invalid.

Sua sponte
SOO-ah SPON-tay;

SOO-ah SPAHN-tee; SOO-ah SPAHN-tay
Action of one's own accord. Action taken without request from another party. For example, a judge may disallow testimony *sua sponte* even if one party fails to properly object.

Subjective

sub-JEHK-tiv

Based on someone's intentions or perceptions. Subjective measures stand in contrast to objective ones, which are based on external facts about the world.

Subject-matter jurisdiction

SUB-jekt MA-tur joo-ris-DIK-shun

A court's power over the nature or type of dispute. Each court's power may be defined by constitutions and statutes. *See* limited jurisdiction, general jurisdiction.

Sublease

SUB-lees

A deal in which a tenant leasing property allows another party to take possession. The original tenant is still liable to the landlord, but the new party must pay an agreed amount to the original tenant.

Subordination

sah-bor-dih-NAY-shun

Placement in a lower rank or position of authority. A subordinate worker is supervised by someone else. A subordinate security interest has lower priority than another security interest.

Subornation

sub-or-NAY-shun

Influence or persuasion to do something unlawful. For example, subornation of perjury means inducing someone to commit perjury.

Subpoena

suh-PEE-nah

Notice for someone to appear for judicial proceedings, backed up by a threatened penalty for not appearing. Also refers to the action of sending a subpoena. People may be subpoenaed into court or a deposition.

Subrogation

SUB-ruh-gay-shun

A way for a party that pays someone's debts to "step into the shoes" of the debtor. The paying party thus acquires some rights of the debtor and can assert these rights in court.

Subscription for shares

sub-SCRIP-shun for SHAY'rs

An offer made to a corporation to buy shares in that corporation. A subscription for shares may be made even before the corporation is formed.

Substantial evidence review

sub-STAN-shul EH-vih-dens reh-VYU

A legal test that applies to fact-finding conclusions of administrative agencies. Such conclusions are valid if reasonably supported by evidence within the agency's field of expertise.

Substantive due process

SUB-sten-tiv dyu PRAH-ses

A requirement that the content of laws cannot unfairly limit individual freedom. A law (or its practical application) may be invalid depending on the individual rights at stake.

Summary judgment

SUM-eh-ree JUH'j-ment

A court's ruling for one party, which may be granted as a matter of law if no genuine issue of material fact is left to be decided at trial.

Summons

SAH-muns

Notice from a court that requires a defendant, witness, or potential juror to appear for proceedings.

Sunshine law

SUN-shai'n law

A type of law that requires more transparent government It forces government bodies to open more meetings and records to the public.

Superseding force

su-pehr-SEE-ding fors

An independent cause of some result that cuts off links between an earlier cause and that result. Someone who murders a tort victim will prevent the original tortfeasor from being liable for the death.

Supplemental jurisdiction

sah-pleh-MEN-tahl joo-ris-DIK-shun

A court's power to hear some claims without express subject-matter jurisdiction because they are closely related to claims over which the court does have independent subject-matter jurisdiction.

Support trust

SAH-port truh'st

A protective trust that forces trustee to pay for certain expenses of the beneficiary, but leaves other decisions in the trustee's discretion. For example, expenses for education and maintenance must be paid.

Suppression hearing

sah-PREH-shun HEE-ring

Procedure used to decide whether to exclude evidence from a criminal trial. Both state and federal exclusionary rules may apply. Most defendants find it very difficult to exclude evidence.

Supremacy Clause

soop-REM-ah-see klawz

Article VI, Clause 2 of the U.S. Constitution. It makes the Constitution, federal statutes, and federal treaties legally superior to any kind of state law.

Surety

SHU-reh-tee

Someone who agrees to be immediately liable for someone else's debt along with the debtor. This differs from a guarantor, who becomes liable only if debtor misses a payment.

Surplus

SUR-plah's

More of something than required to fill a need. A house sold in foreclosure for $50,000 to satisfy $40,000 in loans and fees leaves a surplus of $10,000 for the debtor.

Survival action

sur-VAI-vul AK-shun

A case brought on behalf of a deceased person. Seeks recovery for injuries experienced by the deceased person before death.

Suspect classification

SUS-pekt CLAS-ih-feh-kay-shun

Statutory discrimination based on race, ethnicity, or national origin. Some classifications of aliens are also suspect. Suspect classifications usually need to pass strict scrutiny.

Sustain

sah-STAIN

(1) To rule in favor of something. For example, a judge who agrees with an objection is said to sustain it.

(2) In general, to support something, or continue doing something for a signficant period of time. For example, someone who keeps trying to accomplish a goal is making a sustained effort.

T

Taking

TAY-king

A government's assumption of ownership over private property. A taking may either be possessory (actual), or regulatory (a law susbstantially interferes with the owner's use of the property).

Temporary restraining order (TRO)

TEM-po-rary rest-RAY-ning OR-der (tee ahr oe)

A temporary order that requires or forbids certain action. May be issued before a party has time to seek a preliminary or permanent injunction. Unlike preliminary injunctions, a TRO may be issued without notice to the opposing party.

Tenancy at sufferance

TEH-nan-see at SUH-fe-rens

A type of lease that arises when tenants wrongfully remain in possession of property after a period of lawful possession ends.

Tenancy at will

TEH-nan-see at wil

A type of lease that may be ended anytime, on the wishes of either the landlord or tenant.

Tenancy by the entirety

TEH-nan-see bai thuh en-TAH-yer-tee

Ownership in certain property that is held together by two spouses. It arises automatically in some states whenever property is granted to two spouses in the same document.

Tenancy for years

TEH-nan-see for YEE-arz

A type of lease set to continue for a fixed length of time. The time period can be a year, more than a year, or less than a year.

Tenancy in common

TEH-nan-see in KAH-mun

Ownership in certain property that is held by two or more people. Each person has a distinct interest in the property, and the only joint feature is unity of possession.

Tender

TEN-dur

An offer of performance that meets the requirements of law and contract. Typically, an unconditional attempt to give goods or services. Refusing to accept valid tender may be a breach of contract.

Termination

tur-meh-NAY-shun

The end of some legal relationship. May occur due to an expiration of time, agreement by all parties, unilateral decision by one party, or operation of the law.

Testamentary capacity
teh-stah-MEN(t)-ah-ree kah-PA-seh-tee
Legal ability to make a will. Typical requirements include age of 18, and a mental ability to understand the extent and nature of one's property, its typical beneficiaries, and the distribution being ordered.

Testamentary intent
teh-stah-MEN(t)-ah-ree in-TENT
A wish required to make a valid will. Requires a present intent to dispose of property, only upon death, and as stated in the document alleged to be a will.

Testamentary trust
teh-stah-MEN(t)-ah-ree truh'st
An express trust that is created through a will. It must be created with the same formalities as a will. Assuming validity, it arises upon the testator's death.

Testator
TES-tay-tur
A person who dies having left a valid will. More loosely, a person who makes a will, even if the person is still alive.

Testimonial evidence
teh-steh-MOAN-ee-uhl EH-vih-dens
Evidence that is written, verbal, or otherwise expressed to communicate one's thoughts.

Third-party beneficiary
thur'd PAR-tee beh-nuh-FISH-ary
Someone who benefits from a contract while not actually being a party to it. If the benefits were intentionally given, the third-party beneficiary has legal rights to sue under the contract.

Three-strikes law
th'ree STRA'iks law
A type of law that calls for increased criminal punishment after a repeat criminal's third felony conviction. Also called enhancement statute.

Title
TAI-tl
The combination of all elements that prove legal ownership. The elements include legal right, possession, and custody over property. Also the name given to certificates that evidence such ownership.

Toll
tol
(1) To stop or pause the running of a time limit. For example, a law that extends the statute of limitations given certain conditions is called a tolling statute.
(2) To cancel out or take away. For example, a law might toll the right of certain people to collect lottery

winnings.

Tort
tor't
An unlawful civil harm that is not governed by contract or criminal law. Usually remedied by money damages and sometimes by injunctions.

Tortious interference
TOR-shus in-ter-FEE-rens
(1) Tortious interference with business relationships. Intentional action that persuades one's contracting partner to breach, or otherwise hurts a prospective business relationship.
(2) Tortious interference with family relationships. Injury to someone that allows their spouse or parent to sue for loss of companionship or services.

Trade dress
TRAY'd dres
General look and packaging of a product. Protected from infringement in similar ways as trademarks. Examples include the color, shape, and texture of a wrapper.

Trade secret
TRAY'd SEEK-ret
Any information used in business that is not publicly known or cannot be definitely replicated. Keeping a formula or practice secret is an alternative to patenting it.

Trademark
TRAY'd-mark
A word, phrase, or symbol that distinguishes one brand of product from another. With proper registration, the user of a trademark can get exclusive rights to use it.

Transactional immunity
tran-ZAK-shun-ahl ee-MYOO-nee-tee
Immunity from prosection for any crimes related to the evidence about to be disclosed. For potential criminal defendants, this immunity is better than "use and derivative use" immunity.

Transferred intent
trans-FUR'd in-TENT
A rule that lets judges take defendant's intent to commit unlawful action against someone, and transfer that intent (for legal purposes) to the actual person harmed or action taken.

Transformative mediation
trans-FOR-mah-tiv mee-dee-A-shun
A type of mediation with the primary goal of helping parties better communicate and understand each other's goals. This stands in contrast to immediately trying to find a compromise on a single issue facing the parties.

Transient presence
TRAN-zee-ent PREH-zens
Physical presence in a place, even for a very short time. Such presence in a state is one way for a court to have

personal jurisdiction over someone.

Treason
TREE-zahn
An attempt to overthrow one's government, or to undermine the existence of one's state or country in other ways.

Treasury stock
TREH-zhury STAH'k
Shares in a corporation that were issued to investors, but then bought back by the corporation itself. Goals include lifting up market share prices, and using stock to compensate employees.

Trespass to chattels
TRES-pas too CHAT-els
Intentional act that infringes on one's right to possess his or her personal property. Unlike conversion, not serious enough to order full payment for the item's value.

Trespass to land
TRES-pas too land
Intentional invasion of someone's real property. Defendants are liable for entering the land themselves, or for causing another physical thing to be on the property without permission.

Trial
TRAI-yul
A judicial proceeding with competing parties presenting evidence and legal arguments. A judge then makes a decision, sometimes assisted by a jury.

Trust
truh'st
The holding of legal title to property by one person for the equitable benefit of at least one other person. The person with legal title is a trustee. The other is a beneficiary. Trustees have fiduciary duties to beneficiaries.

Trustee
truh'st-EE
The person who holds legal title to property in a trust. Trustees have fiduciary duties to invest and otherwise manage trust property for the benefit of beneficiaries, who hold equitable title.

U

UCC Article 2
yoo see see AHR-teek'l too
The part of the Uniform Commercial Code that applies to transactions involving goods. It simplifies many deals by providing clear answers to uncertainties.

UCC Article 9
yoo see see AHR-tikl nai'n
The part of the Uniform Commercial Code that applies to security interests. It simplifies secured transactions by providing clear answers to uncertainties.

Ultra vires
ULT-rah VAI-reez
"Beyond powers." Overstepping the bounds of legal authority. *Ultra vires* claims may be made against public officials, and private parties such as a board of directors.

Unavailability
ah-nuh-vey-lah-BIL-eh-tee
Absence. May be actual or constructive. For example, a person who refuses to testify is unavailable for trial. A witness who claims memory loss on an issue is unavailable to be asked about it.

Unclean hands
UHN-kleen HEH'ndz
A defense that claims plaintiff should lose the case because of bad faith. For example, a plaintiff seeking specific performance of a contract should not win if the plaintiff disregarded the contract from day one.

Unconscionability
uhn-KON-shun-abee-leh-tee
An idea that may prevent enforcement of contracts extremely favorable to one party. The goal is to prevent oppression and unfair surprises in fine print.

Undue influence
uhn'DYOO in-FLU-ens
Influence that overcomes someone's free will, and replaces it with the wishes of someone else. Wills executed under undue influence are invalid.

Unenforceable
un-en-FOR-suh-b'l
Legally valid but not subject to enforcement because of some external reason. For example, an oral promise to sell land can be a valid contract. And yet, it typically cannot be enforced due to the Statute of Frauds.

Uniform Commercial Code (UCC)
YOO-nih-form kah-MER-shul KOH-d (yoo see see)

A proposed law that governs sales of goods, secured transactions, and other commercial matters. Adopted and passed with few changes in many U.S. states.

Uniform law

YOO-nih-form law

A proposed law that usually summarizes commonly existing rules on a subject. The goal is to convince state legislatures to adopt the same law and increase uniformity across a legal field.

Unilateral contract

yoo-nih-LAT-eh-rahl KAHN-trakt

Legally enforceable agreement based on one's promise to pay for performance, and the completion of that performance by someone else in return.

Unilateral mistake

yoo-nih-LAT-eh-rahl mihs-TAYK

Mistake of fact by one party to a contract. The mistaken party may be able to void the contract if the other party knew (or had reason to know) of the mistake, and failed to clear it up.

Unjust enrichment

ah'n-JUST en-RICH-ment

Retention of benefits without return payment, if the benefits were provided in good faith and not intended as a gift. Courts may award damages to prevent unjust enrichment despite a lack of enforceable contract.

Unlawful combatant

un-LAW-ful kum-BAT'nt

A person who is not part of the regular military of any recognized state, but who engages in armed conflict against a country or government.

Unsecured

uhn-se-KYOO'rd

Descriptive term for an obligation that is not supported by collateral. Loans without security interests are called unsecured loans. Unsecured creditors accept a higher risk of not recovering debt.

Usage of trade

YOO-sej uhv tray'd

General norms and expectations that come from standards in some commercial field.

"Use and derivative use" immunity

yoo and deh-ree-VAH-tiv yoos ee-MYOO-nee-tee

Immunity from prosecution that stems from evidence about to be disclosed. Once this immunity is granted, a witness can be compelled to testify, and cannot rely on the Fifth Amendment to stay silent.

Utility patent

yoo-TIH-lee-tee PAT'nt

A type of patent issued for a newly invented machine or process that serves some function. Can be useful in any field, such as medicine or industry.

V

Vague

VEY'g

Hazy, imprecise, or poorly defined. A law may be void for vagueness if it fails to give fair notice to reasonable persons of what is permitted and what is not.

Value added tax (VAT)

VAL-yoo A-ded taks (vat)

A charge by the government that is based on how much value is added to goods at each step in their production.

Venire

ven-AY-ree

The full panel of people called in for jury duty. A jury is chosen from this panel.

Venue

VEHN-yoo

A specific designated place. The venue for a case is the location of the courthouse hearing it. Venue may be changed to facilitate accessibility by the parties and the delivery of evidence.

Verdict

VER-dee'kt

A jury's findings on questions of guilt, liability, or fact. General verdicts only state guilt or liability. Special verdicts answer individual fact questions. In a bench trial, a judge's findings of fact may be also be called a verdict.

Vested

VEH's-ted

Definite or complete. Not subject to a condition. For example, a vested future interest in property is one that is certain to ripen given enough time.

Veto

VEE-toh

The power of one branch of government to stop action by another branch. Most commonly refers to a president's refusal to sign a bill into law.

Vicarious liability

vai-KEH-ree-yuhs lah-yah-BIH-leh-tee

Legal responsibility for another person's actions. Stems from a supervisory relationship between the two persons. For example, employer-employee, or parent-child.

Void

VOY'd

Lacking legal effect. If a court finds some contract or law to be void, it had no legal effect from the start.

Void for vagueness
VOY'd for VAY'g-ness

Legal doctrine that makes laws invalid if they are vaguely written. For example, criminal laws must reasonably inform people of what is prohibited and under what circumstances.

Voidable
VOY-duh-b'l

Capable of rightful cancellation by a party. For example, contracting with a child yields a voidable contract. The child may reject this contract upon turning 18 and it will be void without any liability or damages owed.

Voir dire
vu'AR deer

Examination of potential jurors by a judge or lawyer. The goal is to see whether someone may properly and competently serve as a juror. May also refer to the examination of potential witnesses and evidence.

Voluntary dismissal
VAH-luhn-ta-ree dis-MIH-suhl

Official termination of a case, by wish or agreement of the party that started it. Motions to voluntarily dismiss may either result from settlements or decisions to file the case in a different court.

Voluntary intoxication
VAH-luhn-ta-ree in-tahk-sih-KAY-shun

Influence from alcohol or other drugs that are willingly consumed or injected. Can be a defense only to criminal charges that require specific intent.

Voluntary manslaughter
VAH-luhn-ta-ree MAN-slaw-tur

Murder after adequate provocation. In other words, unlawful killing of a person by another, with malice aforethought, but after the victim did something to sufficiently provoke defendant into a sudden rage without time to cool off.

W

Waiver

WAY-vur

Voluntary abandonment of a legal right. Examples include waiver of rights to sue, waiver of one's constitutional rights, and waiver of formal service of court papers.

Waiver of service

WAY-vur uhv SUR-vis

An agreement by someone being sued that he or she received a copy of the complaint, and that formal delivery is not necessary.

Warrant

WOR-ent

(1) An order mandating or permitting action. In criminal law, warrants can be issued to authorize searches, seizures, and arrests.

(2) To guarantee something. A manufacturer may warrant that a product meets certain specifications. A guarantor warrants that another's debts will be paid.

(3) To justify something. For example, misconduct by the prosecution may warrant reversal of a defendant's conviction.

Warrant requirement

WOR-ent

Common name for the Fourth Amendment's prohibition on unreasonable searches and seizures. In truth, warrants are not always constitutionally required for searches and seizures. A better name might be "warrant preference."

Warranty of title and against infringement

WOH-ren-tee uhv tai'tl and ah-GEH'nst in-FRIN-j-ment

A promise by seller that he can rightfully pass title to the goods sold, and a promise that the goods will not give rise to a lawsuit for intellectual-rights infringement.

Waste

way'st

Harm to real property committed by a tenant who does not have indefinite rights to occupy it. Includes harm from neglect as well as unauthorized additions that change the nature of the property.

Watered stock

WHA-t'rd STAH'k

Shares in a corporation that are distributed for free or at a lower price than stated on the stock certificate. Existing shareholders may sue to have watered stock cancelled.

Well-pleaded complaint rule

wel PLEE-ded kahm-PLAINT rool

A requirement that plaintiff's complaint be based on federal law to qualify for federal-question jurisdiction.

Federal law cannot be simply mentioned or expected to have an effect on the case.

Will
wil
Signed document in which one directs how one's property should be distributed upon death. Must be valid where made and where admitted for probate. Typically needs signatures of two witnesses.

Winding up
WAI'n-ding uhp
The process of liquidating and distributing business assets. Must take place before total dissolution of a corporation or partnership.

Wiretapping
wai-yer-TAP'ing
Listening in to private conversations. Often done electronically but may be done manually as well. Must generally comply with the Fourth Amendment.

Witness
WIT-nes
Someone who saw, knows, or can confirm something. Witnesses may be called to testify at trial, in a deposition, or in a written document such as an affidavit.

Writ
rit
A formal order from a public official, commanding someone to do or not do something. Most writs today are written by judges and give orders to other courts.

Writ of *mandamus*
rit uhv man-DAY-muhs
A formal order from a higher court to a lower court or other public official. It compels the recipient to act in accordance with applicable law on some matter brought to the higher court's attention.

Wrongful death
(w)ROWN'g-ful deth
Civil lawsuit seeking compensation from someone who caused another person's death. Damages usually come from loss of support and consortium experienced by the victim's family.

Wrongful institution of civil proceedings
(w)ROWN'g-ful in-steh-TYOO-shun uhv SIH-vil prah-SEE-dings
Putting in motion a civil case against someone, without proper purpose and without probable cause to believe they are truly liable for the wrongs alleged.

Y

"Year and a day" rule

YEE-ahr and a dae rool

A rule that cuts off homicide liability if the victim dies more than a year and one day after injury. This common-law rule has been abolished in many U.S. states.

Younger abstention

YUN-gur ab-STEHN-shun

A way for U.S. federal courts to decline cases if the dispute is already being handled by state institutions, implicates important state interests, and federal constititional issues are not being ignored.

Z

Zoning
ZOW-ning
Application of different land-use and building standards to different parts of a geographic area. Most often done through local legislation on the municipal level.

About Minute Help Press

Minute Help Press is building a library of books for people with only minutes to spare. Follow @minutehelp on Twitter to receive the latest information about free and paid publications from Minute Help Press, or visit minutehelpguides.com.